W9-DBY-422

LITTER

HOW OTHER PEOPLE'S
RUBBISH SHAPES OUR LIVES

Theodore Dalrymple

GIBSON SQUARE

Litter

First published in 2011 by Gibson Square Books

www.gibsonsquare.com

ISBN: 978-1-9-06142-86-5

Printed by CPI Mackays, Chatham ME5 8TD

Contents

Introduction

It is more than four hundred miles from London to Glasgow, and the roadside is strewn practically every yard of the way with litter. I know, because my wife and I recently made the journey.

Many of the trees along the way were hung with plastic bags or tattered remnants of sheets of polythene that flapped in the wind like Buddhist prayer flags on a high Himalayan plain. But it is the grass verges that were most remarkable. For mile after mile they were dappled with detritus: a few pages of newspapers, occasional hubcaps, but overwhelmingly the plastic packaging of refreshments taken by drivers and passengers along the way, and thrown out of the window when finished with. Prominent, in the sense of being very noticeable, were the brightly-coloured cans of soft drinks and the bluish-green translucent plastic bottles of mineral water, that sometimes flashed or sparkled in the sunlight.

It was not only along the motorway that litter flourished, as it were. We took a brief detour to the Lake District, the landscape that so inspired the English Romantics. And indeed the landscape is so hauntingly, even heartbreakingly, beautiful that I, who am deeply averse to romanticism and the self-dramatisation to which it leads, began to feel some sympathy with it. Yet even here the roadside was strewn with litter of precisely the same type; less, it is true, than on the motorway, for the roads are of course much less frequented, but still enough to distract me from the landscape before me.

We drove beyond Glasgow to Loch Lomond: it was the same there. The littering ceased only when we reached the island of Mull.

My wife sometimes suspects me of exaggeration, but she confirmed that my impression was not merely a dyspeptic one or the product of a jaundiced world-view that predisposes me to see only what is wrong with the world and not what is right with it. She confirmed that the amount of litter was, to employ for once justifiably a word that has almost lost its meaning through overuse, incredible.

I have driven long distances through France, Spain, Italy, Germany, Holland, Belgium and other countries in Europe, but I have seen nothing comparable there. I have seen piles of blackened garbage in the streets of Port-au-Prince, and tiny coral atolls in the Central Pacific whose ground was submerged under layers of empty cans of cola, discarded by the overweight islanders who had become miserably dependent on foreign aid for their subsistence. But the condition of Britain is very different from that of Haiti or the atolls of the Pacific; I had never expected my native land to become a vast litter-bin, and for my fellow countrymen to treat it as such.

Rome wasn't built in a day, and Britain wasn't littered in an afternoon. Social, and antisocial, trends do not have clear beginnings like the Big Bang that is said to have founded our universe. For several years I have observed the rising tide of litter in Britain and found it a subject worthy of reflection. Since no one else seemed interested in it, certainly not local councils, I have felt like Autolycus the Rogue, a snapper-up of unconsidered trifles.

My interest in the subject was aroused by walking every day for several years between the general hospital in which I worked in the morning and the prison in which I worked in the afternoon, a distance of a few hundred yards. Since prisons are seldom located in the most select part of towns, it will come as no surprise that the streets through which I walked were poor (though not of course in comparison with some other parts of the world).

In clement and sunny weather, but not in the cold or the rain, the kerbside would glitter prettily with reflections from the tiny shards of glass, in colour between that of aquamarine and peridot, from the smashed side-windows of the cars along the way. Sometimes there were as many as eight collections of such shards by the kerbside: more than one car broken into every hundred yards.

What followed from these observations? In the first instance, the seasonal nature of the break-ins suggested that they were not impelled by sheer poverty or necessitousness, since winter is the season, at least in our climes, of the greatest need.

In the second instance, the sheer number of break-ins, quite unmatched in more prosperous areas, suggested that the poor are more often victims of crime than the rich.

In the third instance, it seemed to me unlikely that all these break-ins were the work, or activity, of many hands. It was much more likely that the person responsible was a production-line worker rather than a skilled artisan turning out in-dividualised products. In other words, here was evidence (if any was needed) that, even in the poorest areas, the class of victims of crime was much larger than the class of perpetrators of crime.

The question frequently came into my mind as to why these considerations, obvious as they were, never seemed to impinge very deeply on the consciousness or feeling of the thinking classes who, when all is said and done, set the tone of our society.

Except for the occasional headless doll or wheel-less pram dumped in the uncut grass of front gardens, the great majority of the litter, like that along the motorway, consisted of the plastic packaging of industrially-produced snacks and drinks. Had I carried out over the years a scrupulous statistical survey of the litter along the way, I should no doubt have been able to discern the evolution of the local taste in junk food; as it was, I noticed in these years the sudden appearance of cans of a drink that was advertised and marketed as energising and restorative after excess, particularly alcoholic excess.

This sudden appearance caused me to ponder the question of whether supply creates demand or demand creates supply. It is true, of course, that people must be aware of the availability of a product before they can desire it specifically: but there are certainly products that are developed to meet some pre-existing need or desire. In this case, however, the appearance of discarded cans of the drink coincided so precisely with an intense advertising campaign, carried out with all available rhetorical resources to mislead, that it was difficult not to see it as a manifestation of commercial manipulation of the population, and an instance of the gullible being gulled.

The attempt to distinguish between a true and a false, or a natural and an unnatural, desire or appetite is probably doomed to failure. For even if raw and natural desires could be shown once to have existed, they could have existed un-contaminated by cultural modification only at the very dawn not of history, but of pre-history. They do not exist now.

What, then, was the source of my irritation at the sudden appearance and rapid dissemination of this new drink with a bright metallic blue, silver and red can to discard? I was about to call the drink worthless, when a question entered my mind like a worm in the bud.

Can anything be worthless that is desired or enjoyed by so many? Was the acquired taste for it any different from my equally-acquired taste for champagne? Was I just a snob? Truly, there is philosophy in litter.

1

The Philosophy of Detritus

Archaeologists deduce a lot from the detritus of ancient civilisations, so why should we not be able to deduce anything from the rubbish of today? And surely what I saw on my way to the prison was eloquent testimony to the way people were living? If you are what you eat, then the packaging of what you eat, and the way that you eat it, is an important part of what and who you are.

The litter changed kaleidoscopically, day by day, as the old was swept away, none too conscientiously, by the council, or blown away by the wind, or removed by the rats, and was always replaced by new. There was never any shortage of litter to examine on my way to the prison.

What did it mean, all this litter? At the very least, it suggested that an Englishman's street is his dining room, as well as his dustbin. Meals are for a Briton (or at least for many Britons) not social occasions, but the furtive and rapid satisfaction of crude appetite. Not only the location, but the content of the meals indicates this. They consist largely of fast foods (the smell of stale fat in which fish or potatoes or chicken have repeatedly been fried is one of the characteristic smells of modern urban Britain). The theory of evolution tells us that man is predisposed by his biological inheritance to like fatty or sugary foods, since they satisfy and sate very quickly, and meals on the African savannah, where man evolved, had to be taken with an eye to dangerous predators or scavengers. If so, it appears that the modern British city is recreating the conditions of the African savannah, full of predators and sca-vengers.

But why do people eat on the street, in so radically unsocial a way? What does it mean that sustenance should be taken in so solipsistic a fashion? Even when people eat in groups on the street, they are not indulging in a social activity, any more than are soldiers marching in formation. They eat rapidly, largely without talking, and get it over with as quickly as possible.

A recent survey found that thirty-six per cent of British children never ate meals at a dining table with other members of their family. Certainly, many of the young men who were my patients in the prison had never in their entire lives eaten a meal at a table with other people. And when, in the course of my medical duties, I visited the homes in the area in which I practised, I was often startled to discover that not only was there no table around which members of households might eat together, but that there was also no evidence of cooking ever having taken place in them. Indeed, they lacked the equipment necessary with which to cook, except for that which had been installed by the builders or landlords of the house. The nearest approach to cooking was the re-heating of prepared meals in a microwave.

I was once at lunch with a free-market economist who claimed that the habit of eating ready-prepared meals was, for the poor at least, an economically rational choice. I said that I very much doubted it, and suspected that he had an ideological commitment to the notion of *homo economicus*, the man who responds to circumstances by means of a rational calculation of economic costs and benefits, and to no other incentives. In response he said that scientific studies had proved it. However, in the area in which I lived at the time there were shops owned and patronised by Asians where it was possible to buy ten kilos of onions for two thirds of the price of one McDonald's hamburger, and other commodities were similarly low-priced. Were Asians economically irrational in shopping there?

I have mistrusted the calculations of economists ever since I visited Rumania in the days of Ceausescu, when economists estimated that economic growth in Rumania had been rapid for many years. Yet there were still no potatoes in the shops, and when on the rare occasions they appeared, a queue, in which people were prepared to wait for several hours, formed at once.

In any case, the economist with whom I spoke assumed that economic rationality was pure rationality. Once it had been established that eating ready meals was the cheapest way to fill a stomach, there was nothing more to be said on the matter. But is it true that if people choose the cheapest means to achieve their ends, their choices are therefore unimpeachable? Is it really true that forty million slobs and slatterns can't be wrong? By extension, that because their choice appears economically rational it is therefore beyond the realm of debate?

But what, in this case, do I mean by wrong? What is a wrong choice when it comes to food? Is not what we eat merely a matter of personal preference and therefore beyond good and evil? Is it not rather a question of accepting that, where choice of food is concerned, as well as in other matters of taste, whatever is, is right? A choice, as Gertrude Stein might have put it, is a choice is a choice. The free market is both morally and aesthetically neutral.

He who seeks in liberty anything other than liberty itself, said de Tocqueville, is destined for servitude. And Macaulay said that if you waited until people were fit to exercise their freedom, no one would ever be free. Those who use the foolishness of other people's choices as a reason for limiting their freedom will forever be extending their own powers.

It is now a commonplace that there are two concepts of liberty, the first positive and the second negative. The latter is merely the absence of external coercion; the former is the fulfilment of the conditions necessary—physical, physiological, psychological, social, economic—for a person to act in a certain way. In other words, you are not free to eat ice cream unless you actually do eat an ice cream. If you fail to eat an ice cream, it is because you were not free to do so in the first place.

From the standpoint of negative freedom, there is nothing to complain of in the way that people choose the food that they eat.

From the standpoint of positive freedom, however, it is quite otherwise. Even if it is not strictly true that no food is available to the (relatively) poor in Britain other than what they do actually eat. Even if their money would easily stretch to other things, even if it were not true that when you add the cost of ingredients to the capital costs of kitchen equipment to those of the gas or electricity necessary to cook and to those of lost opportunities to perform other, more economically valuable tasks (that is to say, their behaviour is economically irrational), it is obvious that their choice is constrained not by their income so much as by their ignorance of alternatives and by their lack of education.

The philosophical problem is that all choices are constrained in this way. The richest or best-informed man does not necessarily know everything. Indeed, the extent of his ignorance is, like that of the poor and uneducated man, infinite. The sum of our knowledge will never equal the sum of our ignorance, either as individuals or as a species. Besides, it is only in retrospect that our choices seem determined; nobody can actually live as if his future choices were predetermined.

Health enthusiasts argue that junk food is bad because of its consequences for health. Such food is rich in ingredients that are said, for the moment at least, to be bad for the body. And certainly the list of ingredients of junk food makes alarming reading even for those who are not particularly health-conscious. Can all those chemicals and additives really be good for us?

But has anyone the duty to live and eat healthily, to choose only those things that are best—that is to say, conduce to the longest possible life—for him? Or to make him do so? In medical ethics these days the principle that is widely held to trump all others is the personal autonomy of the patient, that is to say the right of the patient to decide for himself whether or not to accept the treatment offered him. Save for exceptional circumstances, the doctor has no right to prevail over a patient's will merely because it would be better for the patient if he were so to prevail. And if a patient has a right to refuse antibiotics when he has pneumonia, has anyone the right to deny a person junk food because that person is fat and diabetic?

The analogy is not exact, of course. The doctor may not force what is good upon a patient. But he is under a duty not to offer him anything bad. The grocer has no such obligation, among other reasons because anything taken immoderately is bad. And, in any case, a world in which grocers had such an obligation would be an intolerable one.

The analogy is also not exact because parents, principally mothers, feed their children at a time when they, their children, are utterly dependent upon them. Thus mothers form the taste and habits of their children. Are they, therefore, under an obligation to create healthy habits and tastes? If they were, you'd have to assume habits never change. But they do, both individually and *en masse*. Curry, by way of example, has replaced fish and chips as favourite dish of the British: Indian restaurants are now to be found in many remote villages where it is impossible to find fish-and-chip shops. In any case, official interference in the way mothers feed their children would be a worse evil than the evil it was supposed to prevent.

It might be argued, nevertheless, that a person had a duty to keep himself as healthy as possible when the costs of not doing so were borne, wholly or in part, by others. (Let us assume for a moment that the association between junk food and ill-health is established beyond all reasonable doubt.) After all, no man can both live off junk food and be an anchorite in the Syrian desert. When a man ends up in hospital as a result of his choices, it is almost certain that most of the costs will be borne by people who are complete strangers to him: and thus he has wilfully imposed costs upon them.

But a world in which such an argument were

used to interfere in so intimate and personal a matter as diet would be a world of infinite dictatorship. There are those enthusiasts for public health who never cease to point out that the health of the population improved greatly during the rationing of food made necessary by the Second World War: that those who previously had not eaten enough, or not enough of vital ingredients, now ate well, that is to say adequately from the point of view of nutritional science; while those who had previously eaten too much had their unhealthy surfeiting curtailed. But one has only to imagine a National Diet, laid down, imposed and policed by a Ministry of Nutrition, to shudder. No disease, or at least no disease brought about by the bad choice of food, could be as bad as that.

In any case, diet is far from the only habitual or behavioural factor with deleterious health effects. Sporting activities result in huge numbers of avoidable accidents and injuries that likewise impose costs on others (as they must in any system of healthcare in which there is third-party payment). Why, then, should we single out a particular diet for moral obloquy?

Again, it might be argued that, injuries notwithstanding, the overall health effects of sporting activities are beneficial because of the exercise they entail. But it is not at all clear that the health benefits of exercise could not be dissociated from the risks of injury, if not wholly, then very largely. If it is retorted that sport has non-health benefits, such as the enjoyment it gives to participants, this is a retort that the consumers of junk food could also return.

Moreover, it is possible that, by dying early, consumers of junk food are actually performing a valuable service for their fellow-citizens. They are helping to increase the ratio of economically-active to non-active citizens, no mean consideration in the time of a rapidly ageing population. This, certainly, had been argued with regard to smokers, though with a slight difference: throughout their smoking careers, smokers contributed very greatly to the exchequer. However, there is considerable overlap between smokers and consumers of junk food.

If the health consequences of a diet of junk and ready-prepared food do not allow us to condemn it, what does or could do so?

Culinary aesthetics hardly seem sufficient grounds. Not only because the canons of taste are so variable, but even if they could be established on an indubitable basis, those who offended against them would be offending aesthetically, not morally. The connection between moral and aesthetic judgement is not a simple one. Truth is not beauty, and beauty is not goodness. Of course, if like Nero you spill human blood on grass just because you like the juxtaposition of red and green, morality enters the question. But however much one might be repelled by a man who wore a grass-green shirt with blood-red trousers, one could not deduce moral failing from it.

The wrongness of a diet of junk food, it seems to me, inheres in something that is not absolutely intrinsic to it. It is not so much what is in the diet, bad and unhealthy as this may be in many respects, that is wrong, but how and why the diet is taken. For the diet is a metonym for a way of life, a way of life that is not merely unattractive, but productive of much evil in the form of avoidable suffering.

The litter in the streets on the way from the hospital to the prison indicated a profoundly unsocial way of eating, and, hence, of life itself. This is of the greatest possible significance.

2

The Family Meal

How do the people live who discard this litter, who let it fall where it listeth, that is to say whenever they have finished consuming the contents that it wraps? Sometimes, of course, they do not even finish the contents, but leave them half-eaten by the kerb. There are few less appetising sights.

What is the family upbringing that has socialised, or anti-socialised, these habitual litters to behave in this way?

For the most part, they thave been raised in households with a shifting membership, where the mother is the only reliably present figure. Fathers, or more accurately inseminators, are almost wholly absent, having little more to do with their offspring than does a bull with his once he has serviced the cows to the farmer's satisfaction. Occasionally such a father might appear bearing a pair of shoes for a child of his, conscioius that he is thereby going well beyond what is expected of him, and in reality to gain further sexual access to his baby-mother (as he calls her in his more genteel and less vituperative moments). Such visits often end in conflict or violence, because the mother now has a new baby-father, who, not surprisingly, does not want previous baby-fathers to remind him of what he regards as her infidelity before she ever met him. It is now almost an indelicate question to ask a child or young person who has grown up in such an environment who his father is. More than once my enquiry was answered, 'Do you mean my father at the moment?'

In such households—and there are now so many of them that they cannot be regarded as abnormal, at least in the statistical sense—meals are not taken at regular times, or with others around a table.

There are several reasons for this. The adult male of the household, if there is one, will not consent to tie himself down to, or be tied down by, any routine that he believes will limit his freedom. He will foreclose upon any chance that might arise. Routine is for bores and slaves, and makes for a dull life. The man of the household may not have read much of the literature of the romantics, but their ideas have filtered down to him by social osmosis. Freedom for him is nothing but the ability to respond to whim whenever and wherever it occurs; anything that inhibits the expression of whim is tyranny.

There is another reason why so many males of such households will not conform to regular mealtimes. Many of them are extremely jealous and the irregularity of their returns to the household serves a dual purpose, first of surveillance (always more effective when random and unpredictable), and second of keeping him constantly in the forefront of the mind of the woman, who is left wondering when he will turn up. This has the merit, from the point of view of the jealous man, of excluding thoughts of other men from her mind.

Such jealousy is inflamed, for obvious reasons, in situations in which relations between the sexes are fluid, impermanent and unconstrained by any sense of obligations that can be relied on rather than picked at. The evidence of the impermanence of the woman's affection — in the form of children by previous 'partners' — is inescapably before the man. It takes no great powers of inductive reasoning to work out that what happened to them, the previous partners, might soon happen to him. Indeed, it quite often happens that the man demands that the premonitory evidence of future infidelity to him, that is to say her previous children, should be expelled from the household; a demand that is met by sending them to their grandmother's, if they have not yet reached the age of fending for themselves—that is to say fifteen or sixteen. Such a man often demands that a meal should be ready for him as soon as he returns to the household, though he refuses to say when that will be. This is not a demand propitious to disciplined cooking.

It is hardly surprising, in the circumstances, that the man and woman seldom eat together, let alone with the other members of the household. The woman, who eats alone, is unlikely to cook for herself, even if she knows how (after a generation or two of living like this, there is little reason why she should know).

What, then, of her children? How do they learn to eat?

The woman is often very young and not very mature even for her age. As likely as not, she thought a child would solve the problems of her life: boredom, lack of purpose, and even difficulties with the boyfriend who is to be the father of the child. And at first a baby does seem a solution, at least to the first two of these problems. The baby, brought forth in pain and sorrow, seems at first an achievement rather than a natural phenomenon. It is therefore a source of pride, especially as he or she draws for a time the attention of others. Unfortunately, however, the baby grows and becomes more difficult to handle. The tasks of love become more difficult and demanding, more fraught with ambiguities and contradictions. The problem of boredom returns, only this time it is a busy boredom. Often, illogically, another baby seems the answer, to recapture the glory days of the one before. But of course it only compounds the difficulties in the end. Furthermore, two, three or four former boyfriends, all jealous though none faithful, make trouble for her, and together with the constant attention her children now need, her life becomes a torment of anxiety. It is small wonder, then, that she does not so much train a child in its eating habits as surrender to its demands for the sake of a quiet life in the short term.

When a child wants food, therefore, the mother wants to satisfy it as quickly and painlessly as possible. She certainly does not want any trantrums, much less prolonged struggles over diet (my wife's sister once refused to eat her spinach by keeping it in the pouches of her cheeks for more than twelve hours). The simplest way of procuring a fast peace is to give the child exactly what it wants.

Alas, what the child wants, and what is most attractive to him, is not necessarily what is best for him. Left to his own devices, he will choose sweet and fatty foods. A taste for variety is mostly acquired, not inborn. It is one of the tasks of parenthood to mould a child's tastes, and if that moulding does not take place his tastes will remain those of a child. And this is so in fields other than that of diet. Subtlety, discrimination and so-phistication are not innate, nor do they develop spontaneously.

Rather than train the child, which inevitably involves difficulties, struggles and even conflicts, the mother opts for an easy life. That is why you often see mothers in shops and supermarkets asking children as young as three what they would like for their next meal. They are negotiating difficulties later in the day.

Authority is thus transferred from adult to child. The latter comes to believe that his own whim is law. Of course, this lays up future conflict with authority as treasure in heaven when, as is inevitable, he finds his whims thwarted or disregarded by it. In prison, when I refused the request, or rather the demand, of a prisoner for a medication that I deemed he did not need, he would often exclaim, 'No! What do you mean, no?'

as if hearing a word for the first time in his life.

Once the child is old enough to fend for himself in the confines of the home, the mother abdicates responsibility for his meals, apart from buying the food which enters the house and which she deposits in the refrigerator. The child learns to forage: to find food whenever he feels like it and to take what he wants. His meals are solitary, brutish and short—though they may very well be frequent.

This pattern of eating is disastrous in its consequences. It deprives the child of one of the most powerful, and relatively painless and ultimately enjoyable, lessons in how to live with others. He both learns a bad lesson and fails to learn a good one.

The habit of eating in concert with other members of the family (or household) teaches several important things. Because the child takes his meals at times not decided by himself, he learns that his internal state—his appetite of the moment—is not the only consideration in the question of whether to eat or not to eat. Sometimes he will eat when he is not hungry, and sometimes he will not eat when he is. Above all he will learn that eating is not merely a biological but a social activity. In other words, he will learn a lesson in self-control for the sake of those with whom he lives: an essential component, incidentally, of self-respect.

A child that does not learnt to eat in concert with others learns precisely the opposite lessons. His appetite determines all. If he feels like it, he eats, and if he does not feel like it, he doesn't eat. At any rate, he has no reason to consult the wishes or convenience of others in making his decision. Furthermore, he may even fail to appreciate that he is making a decision at all, since an appreciation that is making a decision requires that one experiences a potential conflict between one desire or impulse and another. It is small wonder that those who do not early experience this potential conflict within themselves are very soon prey to various addictions, or repetitively self-destructive acts, without realising that their behaviour involves a choice on each and every occasion. They ascribe what they do to anything or anybody but themselves.

No principle, then, is involved in the decision as to when, where and how to eat. The child becomes crudely hedonistic and egotistical, for whom all frustrations of appetite are unjustified exercises of power by external agencies. When he does not get what he wants, he becomes fractious, aggressive and even violent, and blames someone else. No, indeed. What do you mean, no?

Again, it is hardly surprising that those who eat in this fashion—by foraging and grazing—eat on the street. The satisfaction of crude appetite is what they seek because it is what they know. The circle between their upbringing and litter on the street is closed.

3

The Degree Class

It should not be thought, however, that the pattern I have described is confined to the lowest stratum of British society: far from it. If it were, litter would be largely confined to the poorest areas, but it is not, as I have already remarked.

While I was teaching a group of students, the subject of self-control came up. The students were alert and intelligent. In the ensuing discussion, I mentioned that when I was young to eat on the street was still regarded as a somewhat degraded thing to do. The students laughed at this instance of quaint, outmoded and ridiculous gentility. They could see no reason whatever for such a strange taboo. I realised that they, too, ate on the street.

This was confirmed when I walked in an area of the city inhabited largely, if not exclusively, by students. It would hardly be an exaggeration to say that I had to wade through the rubbish on the pavement, all of it wrappings of fast food consumed on the street on the way home. One of the advantages of the British class system is that it enables you to tell a person's class by the way he speaks; and it was clear from the speech of the students whom I heard as I waded through this mess that they were middle-class. There was not a proletarian among them.

It would be an elementary error to ascribe the blame for the mess to the food rather than to the people who ate it and then discarded its packaging in much the same way as a cow defecates in a field and blame the grass. Shortly afterwards, I visited a university town in America, where students were inclined to eat the same kind of disgusting food as their British counterparts. But the streets of the town were not strewn with litter. On the contrary, they were extremely clean. Litter does not strew itself, it has to be strewn.

What, then, accounts for the difference in the behaviour of the British and American students in this regard? It might be, of course, that the American students were just as bad as the British, but that the American town council was far more assiduous and efficient in clearing up after them. However, I do not think this could be the explanation. Rather than a visible army of street cleaners in the American town, the streets of the American town were cleaner because the

American students were cleaner.

I am sure that most British students would express a tender concern for the environment. Many of them will discourse fluently and perhaps with passion on global warming, on carbon emissions, on the unsustainability of our current industrial and agricultural practices, on the destruction of global biodiversity, of the finitude of fossil fuel, of the disappearance of the rain forest, of the meting of the icecaps and the consequent travails of the polar bears, of the rising of the sea level and the threatened extinction of coral atolls, of the chemical poisoning of the earth and its atmosphere, and so forth. Not a few would probably subscribe to the neo-Pagan notion of Gaia, of the whole biosphere as a kind of transcendent organism.

Paradoxically, the mess directly around them— particularly the one they had helped themselves to create—raises no concern. They would blame greed for the state of the world, not their own or that of 'ordinary' people, but that of corporations in particular and of capitalism in general. They would argue, say, that the increase in packaging and plastic bags was to blame, driven by a nefarious profit motive (which was unknown to them, of course). Corporations and the people who owned or managed them have no regard for the long-term consequences for mankind and the planet. What the world needed, therefore, was control by those who understood the workings of the biosphere—people, in fact, like them.

The contrast between this rhetoric and the actual conduct of the students could hardly be greater, and it is symptomatic of a great change in the national character. As the Americans still are, so the British used once to be a pragmatic people, more interested in the concrete than in grand abstractions, in practice than in theory. But the spread of tertiary education, and the increased public exposure, prominence and importance of those with a degree as a new class has affected a great change that the Americans, perhaps because of the sheer size, diversity and economic momentum of their country, have in large part avoided. They remain an intensely practical people, whose main interest in theories is the results that they bring. In Britain, by contrast, theorising has become the handmaiden of resentment, recrimination and the search for the explanation of personal dissatisfaction, and thus the source of an often very twisted form of gratification.

The expansion of tertiary education did not occur in mainly technical subjects, but rather in those that encouraged abstract thought about human behaviour and conduct. The nature of this thought was 'critical,' not in the sense that, say, A. C. Bradley was a critic of Shakespeare, but critical in the sense of examining everything from the standpoint of a purely theoretical perfection, a standpoint from which, not surprisingly, everything that existed was found severely wanting and therefore of very little worth.

The Whig interpretation of history, in which the benighted past is considered but a stage towards the enlightened present, has largely been replaced by an equal and opposite miserabilist historiography, according to which the past is nothing but the historical cause of our present discontents. An expanding intelligentsia, after all, needs an expanding number of deeply-rooted social problems to justify its existence and pre-eminence. It therefore feels called upon to emphasise not the achievements, but the follies and crimes of history. Obviously, what has been produced by folly and crime cannot be worthy of care, let alone preservation. The world must be made anew.

The question to be answered in this new intellectual climate was not where wealth, but where poverty came from, as if mankind had been born into riches that had somehow dissipated. The blame for this unnatural poverty had to be placed somewhere, and the most obvious place was the rich and powerful of all ages and of all places. The illicit wealth of some was always the unjust poverty of most.

It need hardly be said that criticism of wealth and power (often justified, of course) is not incompatible with a desire to become rich and powerful oneself. But it does make it difficult to acknowledge such a desire, and therefore introduces into the soul a strong motive for self-deception, to say nothing of the deception of others. Envy is a vice that threatens to ensnare us all, and the frank recognition of its siren call to us is the only way to control it. By contrast, the supposition that one is motivated by pure and disinterested benevolence, by a desire only to improve the world, serves to disguise from oneself other motives that, though inevitable, do not flatter our self-conceit.

In the United States, thanks to a religiosity that is not always attractive, the notion of original sin is still popular. But in Britain, where religion is practically dead save at the margins of society, mankind has converted *en masse* to self-worship. If men do bad things it is because something has perverted them from their original goodness; and since most men are partial to themselves, and easily blind themselves to their own voluntary faults, they locate their own evil elsewhere than in their hearts. It is social and economic structures that are bad, not they themselves; for them, a society that is so perfect that they would have to make no effort to be good is not only possible but the only thing really worth aiming at.

In this kind of thinking about the human condition, abstractions become more real than the concrete reality by which one is surrounded. Exploitation, oppression and so forth are more vividly present in the mind than one's immediate physical and social environment.

It hardly matters in the face of such abstractions how one behaves oneself. This is because abstractions are so big and one's conduct is so small. Nothing that I do, beyond agitating in concert with others for a perfect world, makes any difference to the state of the world, given the vastness of the forces ranged against me. Therefore, I can do what I like until such time as the structure of the world brings about perfection. Before that state of perfection, the exercise of virtue is meaningless; after it, automatic.

In the meantime, of course, I must hold the right opinion, and perhaps even protest from time to time. To do so is the beginning, and also the end, of virtue in our current circumstances. To be good, one does not have to act well; one has to think and express the right opinions, and express them as vehemently as possible.

There is thus no contradiction between a deep concern for the environment and strewing the world with litter.

A few days after treading through the litter left by students, I happened to spend a few days in Eastbourne, a town on the South Coast of England much-derided for its faded gentility, to which the more prosperous of the petit bourgeoisie go to die in peace and tranquillity, tended (increasingly) by foreign nurses.

Mockery apart, the sea walk along the coast is of great beauty, and I walked it several times. It was at a season of the year when it was not crowded, but there were nevertheless a sufficient number of elderly people, both couples and alone, who strolled in the sunshine or sat on the benches facing out to sea.

By then, the phenomenon of litter and its meaning was, if not uppermost in, at least near the very forefront of my mind. For that reason, perhaps, something struck me forcibly, something that is, on reflection, most unusual in the Britain of our time: that all along the sea walk, where the old people strolled and sat, there was not a single piece of litter, not for two or three miles.

The people who did not litter the sea walk were not striving to save the planet, and probably would hardly have been aware of the Gaia 'hypothesis.' Ecology probably meant nothing to them, either as a word or as a concept. On the contrary, they were simply behaving in what they would have considered a normal fashion. If asked why they did not drop litter—though the very question would have seemed extremely strange to them— they would no doubt have referred to the convenience, the wishes of others. But, finally, not dropping litter was for them no more a carefully thought-out choice than dropping litter was for the students.

Perhaps someone, discomfited by the alarming change in habits of people in Britain, would say that the change in question is simply the effect of age. I do not think so: when I look into the faces of those living in Eastbourne, I do not think, 'In your youth you dropped litter, and only now have you stopped doing so.' They do not drop litter, because they never dropped litter.

Other countries have undergone the same social evolution as Britain, and yet one still sees more litter in a hundred yards in Britain than in a hundred miles in theirs. Something else than that social evolution, then, must explain the litter in Britain.

All explanations of complex social phenomena remain speculative because history provides few controlled experiments (and even controlled experiments are often susceptible to different interpretations). But perhaps the first thing to establish is that there really has been an increase in the littering of Britain, that it is not just a false perception of me personally or a manifestation of what the professionally complacent like to call 'a moral panic,' that I am not just someone lamenting the passing of time. There does, after all, seem to be a tendency to see the past through rose-coloured spectacles that are hard-wired into the brain.

So what is the proof? My own memory of cleaner streets is insufficient because of the fallibility of human memory. Memory, like reason, is the slave of the passions, as scientific experiment demonstrates. Melancholic or depressed people, for example, remember the past in accordance with their present mood of despondency, attributing to it the misery they feel in the present. When I say, then, that Britain is more littered than it was, why should anyone believe me who is not himself already convinced of it? Clearly, I have an axe to grind, and I wouldn't pretend otherwise.

I am not alone, however, in my perception.

Many others have noticed the same thing, and while collective hallucination and delusion is possible, I do not think this is an example of it. Memory may be fallible, but it is fallibly, rather than invariably, fallible: in other words, sometimes it is accurate. In particular, the phenomenon has been noticed by people with no axe to grind, namely intermittent visitors to our shores who have no emotional involvement in the matter. A French cousin of mine by marriage, who had visited many countries, made a remark on her first visit to Britain that stuck in my mind: 'I thought,' she said, 'that England was a northern country and therefore would be clean.' On the contrary, she was surprised by its filth.

Ever since my interest in the subject developed, I scan old photographs of ordinary street scenes in Britain for litter. After all, you could hardly point a camera now in any direction in the country and not capture evidence of littering. And the fact is that, in photographs of times gone by, you rarely see any litter at all.

Of course, photographs in former times took far longer to take than they do now, and anyone who wanted to resist my conclusion might argue that early photographs were staged rather than the instantaneous capture of scenes such as they are nowadays. And perhaps photographers, in an age less concerned to capture the actual grittiness of real life than we are now, declined to take scenes that were 'spoiled' by litter, and even arranged for cleaning before they photographed.

Perhaps: but I rather doubt it. In particular I have scoured street scenes in which there were many people going about their ordinary business, and it seems to me unlikely that they could have been arranged to exclude the appearance of litter in them.

Ah, perhaps there was no litter—say those who do not want to recognise the increase as real, but want it to be an artefact of selective memory—but in those day people had nothing to throw away. In other words, they were too poor to throw away even a scrap of paper, let alone tons of the stuff as they do now. And plastic and polystyrene weren't even invented then.

These tactics have been used before by people who argued first that there had been no increase in crime, the apparent but not real increase being an illusion created by the improved efficiency with which crime was reported (for example, because people had greater access to telephones); but then, when the denial became unsustainable and even ridiculous, they argued that the reason that theft and other forms of dishonesty had increased was because there was so much more to steal. Where poverty had once been the favoured explanation of criminal behaviour, affluence now became the culprit. In short, any argument that came to hand was advanced to avoid painful reflection on the change in the very conduct and character of people that some aspect or other of modernity had wrought.

The argument that an absence of litter bespeaks poverty has, in fact, been used. An American photographer called Jean-Maire Simon published a book of photographs in the 1980s about Guatemala. The country was then in the throes of a brutal civil war that pitted a conservative government, controlled very largely by the army, against a revolutionary guerrilla movement. In common with most foreigners who interested themselves at the time in the affairs of Central America, the photographer sympathised wholeheartedly with the guerrillas. (With the end of the civil wars in the isthmus, and the defeat of the various guerrilla movements that carried the utopian yearnings of western intellectuals with them, interest in the region has declined virtually to nil.)

The book of photographs was a work of propaganda of the four-legs-good, two-legs-bad variety. And in truth it was not very difficult to make such propaganda because the government side did indeed commit many acts of brutality. But among the photographs was one of a central plaza of a small Guatemalan town called Rabinal. And the fact that there was not a single piece of litter to be seen was used by the author in her caption as evidence of the extreme poverty of the townspeople (and therefore, by implication, a justification for the guerrilla movement which, only too predictably, had brought so much misery and death in its wake). She quotes the anthropologist, Pierre van den Berghe, writing in the 1960s:

> One of the surest indices of the poverty... is the almost complete absence of paper as refuse. True, the streets are kept very clean, though all unpaved, and they are regularly swept. But even after the market, while the ground is littered with leaves used in wrapping, hardly a scrap of paper is visible. Paper is simply not refuse here.

Why was the lack of litter, more than twenty years later when the country was in fact considerably richer, not evidence of the cleanliness and social self-discipline of the townspeople? One would hardly ascribe the neatness of Switzerland to the poverty, at any rate the material poverty, of its inhabitants, quite the reverse in fact. The author did not want to admit of this possibility because it would be tantamount to an admission that the townspeople had a municipal pride. If they had such a pride, then all could not be for the worst in Guatemala, and therefore the civil war that the guerrillas had quite deliberately started, was unjustified. The absence of litter would then make the guerrillas not the heroes but the villains of the piece.

Several people to whom I broached the subject of the increase in litter in Britain at once suggested that it was caused by the possession of more to throw away. They were all educated, and perhaps such an explanation could have occurred only to the educated: for it takes years of training to be able effortlessly to disregard the obvious by coming up with a theory so bogus. People have always had enough to make a mess, and they do not make a mess in proportion to their income or standard of living.

Why, then, do so many educated people feel the necessity to transfer responsibility *in toto* for a phenomenon such as littering from the people who do it to the inanimate objects with which it is done, or failing that, to some vast and impersonal forces almost beyond individual human comprehension?

I suspect that it is because of a desire to preserve democratic sentiment that, in reality, is only tenuously held or believed in. It is obvious that littering is not the work, if I may call it such, of the few, but of the many. A few people could not possibly have produced the results that have been obtained. Even if they had devoted their entire lives to the deliberate desecration of the landscape, the few would not have been able to do so. Hundreds of thousands of people at least, and probably millions, must have participated in the littering. Hence, to blame litterers is to blame a substantial proportion of the population.

In the modern world, this is not permissible. To suggest that ordinary people can behave badly of their own volition is to mark oneself out as an Enemy of the People. Therefore some force acting upon them, without their knowledge, must be found to exculpate them. The exculpation removes from the exculpator all suspicion of harbouring un- or anti-democratic sentiments.

To blame the wrapping rather than the unwrapper serves this purpose admirably. It opens the way to safely impersonal reflection upon the commercial forces that have led to so much of our food being wrapped in what subsequently becomes litter. It distracts us from the cardinal fact that in other countries, where the same commercial forces have led to the same or similar ways of packaging food, at least to the extent of permitting people to litter the countryside if they were so inclined, the level of littering is incomparably lower. And thus we are not forced to reflect upon the behaviour of some of our fellow men. We can maintain the illusion that they are the victims of something other than bad character.

4

Gin Lane

But bad character leading to bad behaviour, arising from bad principles, does not develop spontaneously. It must have some explanation beyond Original Sin, that is to say beyond a flaw in man's essential make-up. We are not, after all, considering men as they were in a state of nature, before the invention (or development) of culture and civilisation. The litterers are the children and grandchildren of men who did not carelessly sow the land with their detritus as and when they felt like it.

Part of the problem, I suspect, is the cult of spontaneity and authenticity. Where man's nature is believed to be inherently good, his first impulses will be believed to be blameless. It is only when he begins to reflect consciously upon his own impulses, letting them be modified by the corrupting processes of culture and civilisation, that he does harm. And Britain was probably more susceptible to the cult of spontaneity than other countries because, since the Victorian age at any rate, its culture valued self-restraint above almost any other quality. To display emotion in public, even when the provocation to do so was great, was a sign of weakness and unmanliness. Everyone admired, and came to expect, stoical or ironical acceptance of misfortune or even catastrophe. Spontaneity—the giving way to the emotion of the moment—was frowned upon as being the behaviour of lesser people than the British, of people without the law.

The cult of restraint was not incompatible with sentimentality, and perhaps even required it as an outlet. A man who had difficulty in expressing affection for his own children might easily become tearful over a dog or a scene from Dickens. But the cult also encouraged an ironical attitude to the world, as a means of detaching oneself from one's own suffering. To discount one's own travails on the grounds of their smallness by comparison with the size of the world enabled people to keep their dignity in the face of personal disaster.

This emotional restraint—a departure for the British, who had previously been known for violent and ungovernable emotionality—was common to all classes. Of course not everyone shared it. No cultural trait is ever shared by everyone who is born into and grows up in that culture. Still, it was a recognisable trait. My mother, arriving as a refugee from Germany in 1939, recognised and admired it; so did my wife, arriving from France thirty years later. It was clearly recognisably present as I grew up—I admired and aspired to it also—but it declined with rapidity.

When I was very young, the plays of Terence Rattigan, who had been the most prominent and popular playwright of his time, and whose plays assumed an understanding of emotional restraint in their audience, suddenly went out of fashion, in a year or two; John Osborne's *Look Back in Anger* suddenly made Rattigan's emotional and intellectual dilemmas seem not merely old-fashioned, but positively antediluvian. In retrospect, it is not easy to discern exactly, or even approximately, the characters in Osborne's play were angry about, but that is precisely the point. Strong emotion had become self-justifying, a good in itself. It did not have to be attached to anything in particular, it had only to be genuinely and authentically felt. Since to have feelings is a fact and since feelings are neither true nor false, at least in the cognitive sense, and also in the romantic conception of them, they were all equally 'valid.' Validity, not in the sense of the formal logical coherence of an argument, but in the sense of an opinion genuinely and sincerely held, even if all the available evidence was against it, replaced truth as the touchstone by which a statement was to be judged. This, of course, is deeply irrational both in its presumptions and effects.

Reading four volumes of Harold Pinter's plays—the man who in large part has assumed Rattigan's mantle as the most popular playwright of his age—I did not find in all the hundreds of pages a single discussion of weight. Man does not live by logic or intellectual conversation alone. But he does sometimes indulge in them. It is true that much human discourse is not a debate as a matter of form, and most people do not spend much, let alone most, of their time discussing and refuting the ideas of others in a more or less coherent fashion. But there is no requirement for playwrights, even naturalistic ones, to imitate human life exactly—indeed, there is no possibility of it. We do not expect characters on the stage to spend a third of their time asleep. A map that exactly reproduced the features of what it mapped would be a replica, not a map. It is precisely selectivity, that faculty that is half-instinctive and half-conscious, that endows literature with meaning. Human life cannot be led wholly irrationally any more than it can be led wholly rationally.

An entire culture does not change because the work of one playwright, however eminent, succeeds another; indeed, Osborne and Pinter might have been as much a symptom of change as a cause of it. But that there was a change, and a pretty swift one, it is scarcely possible to doubt.

The weakness of the old British culture, its vulnerability, was that its charms were subtle, discreet and far from obvious. Sometimes they were so subtle that even their existence was in doubt.

These charms were certainly not hedonistic. As the Hungarian humorist and refugee to Britain, George Mikes, observed, even the rich in Britain did not necessarily live in comfort, but rather wore down-at-heel clothes and sat among draughts. 'The continentals,' he said, 'have good food, the English have good table manners;' or again, 'The continentals have sex, the English have hot water bottles.' (When I was growing up, they needed them.) In such a climate, it was all to easy to long for the blushful Hippocrene.

A little book published in France in the 1950s, in the series *Que sais-je?*, called *La vie anglaise* (*English Life*), remarked upon how almost everything said by an Englishman was infused with irony and had a double meaning. 'We must meet again soon' really meant 'I hope never to clap eyes on you again.' French anglophiles, such as André Maurois, had noticed the same thing many years earlier, and saw in it not duplicity, but an admirable self-restraint that facilitated civilised intercourse.

The subtle charms of the old culture are perhaps best caught obliquely in the crime novels of the so-called golden age (there are golden ages in literature, if not in life). No nation has ever so successfully turned murder into a comedy of manners, itself a considerable feat of irony. In the novels are caught all the petty snobberies, social gradations and mildly bogus gentility of English, and Scottish, life as it once was. It is difficult now to write such novels because the culture has changed so completely, into something much cruder, but also more sophisticated, and the sense of being consciously disabused about everything.

Subtlety is always at the mercy of crudity, and restraint of hedonism. In addition, Britain found itself after the war in an unenviable position: unenviable, that is, for people who think that the exercise of power is essential to the good life. For the first time in two centuries, Britain was reduced from a world power to a smallish offshore island, a second-rate power struggling even to remain second-rate.

Those who, had they been born a generation or two earlier, would have bestridden the world like colossi, and decided the fate of whole nations, were now reduced by exchange control to carrying no more than £25 with them when they went. The contrast, then, with their immediate predecessors could hardly have been more obvious or more painful. And they had not even the consolation of good food or good weather to fall back on.

A generation was born that had, or thought it had (which is more important), no reason to be attached to the culture of its parents that had brought about such precipitous and humiliating decline.

Of course, it did not recognise disappointment as a motive for its rejection of the culture that it had inherited. Like all reformers, it was better, happier, freer world that it claimed to be trying to bring about. And some of that generation were indeed very talented satirists and social critics. They brought about something of a cultural switch. What had previously been regarded as desirable was made to look ridiculous, and what had previously been looked down upon (as vulgar or degraded) was elevated as liberating and health-giving.

Such values as restraint, understatement, modesty and a preference for the implicit were replaced by their opposites. No such change occurs overnight, of course. It took years for the change to work its way through the country and even now pockets of resistance remain. But when Mr Blair said, of the outpouring of surface emotion that followed the death of Princess Diana in a sordid road accident, 'that we have found a new way of being British,' he was only saying something that was obviously true. As a populist, of course, he gave a positive moral evaluation to this truth (for him the word 'new' was automatically a seal of approval). It takes a certain depth, after all, to be able to perceive shallowness.

We are all King Lear now, unable or unwilling to distinguish between emotion and the expression, or rather the exhibition, of emotion. The Duke of Kent's rebuke to Lear, warning him against taking Cordelia's refusal to match her sisters' high-flown declarations of filial love as a sign of indifference, would now mean nothing to us:

> They are not empty-hearted
> Whose words reverb no
> hollowness.

Restraint, then, was out, and self-expression was in, together with spontaneity; and the new was good because the old was bad.

One of the results of the espousal of self-expression and spontaneity as good in themselves regardless of what was actually expressed thereby, was mass public drunkenness of the type that is to be seen inb the cities, towns and even villages of Britain on Friday and Saturday nights. There the young regularly enact scenes of drunken debauchery that they impose a virtual curfew on all those who do not wish to take part in them.

I discovered from experience that you can never raise the subject in educated company in Britain without someone piping up, usually with a considerable degree of self-satisfaction, about Hogarth's *Gin Lane*, that is to say the drunken debauchery in Britain in the mid-eighteenth century soon after the introduction of cheap distilled liquor—gin into the country. In other words, 'twas ever thus, and if 'twas ever thus, it must be all right and there is therefore nothing to worry about.

It is boring, though regrettably necessary, to refute obvious and (I suspect) wilful error. Hogarth was a moralist appalled by Gin Lane who condemned what he saw as strongly as he was able, in the hope of effecting some change for the better. Moreover, it is an historical fact that things did change for the better, at least if moderation is preferable to excess, between 1743, when Hogarth's print was first published, and the latter part of the Twentieth Century.

Therefore, those who see in the current scenes of mass public drunkenness nothing but a continuation of Gin Lane rely, in an unstated way, upon a theory of genetic atavism or throw-back that is little short of absurd, and not supported in the slightest by genetic science. Once again, the desire to avoid the disturbing thought that ordinary people can behave badly en masse leads at least some intellectuals to rationalise, in this case by denying that a problem really exists because it has always existed, and what has always existed is not a real problem.

There are, of course, explanations of the mass public drunkenness in British towns and cities other than the collective loss of self-control that I invoke. They are not alternative explanations, however, in the sense of being in complete contradiction to my favoured explanation. For example, there is the price of alcohol. When the price goes down, the consumption goes up (classical economics would expect this of ever commodity). And indeed, the price of alcohol has declined markedly in terms of labour-time necessary to procure it, heavy taxation notwithstanding. Discretionary incomes have risen at precisely the time when discretion itself has fallen.

Moreover, licensing regulations have been progressively eased. It used to be forbidden for there to be an agglomeration of bars within a small area, but now it is not only permitted but seems to be positively encouraged. Not only the number, but the size of the bars has increased. Many of them will accommodate hundreds and even thousands of people. The noise generated in them is so great (to which agitating music is superadded) that the notion of a quiet social drink accompanied by conversation becomes laughable. Thus everyone drinks in them faster and more, almost in competition with one another.

But the cheapness of alcohol notwithstanding, and the size and character of the bars also, the question remains as to why hundreds of thousands and perhaps millions of young Britons should choose to behave in the way that they do? Why should they not only go to these bars, but regard doing so as the high point of their existence, to which they look forward longingly? Why should they gather in such large herds, in which the render themselves incapable of the distinguishing speech, the one thing that makes us human?

They do so specifically to have an excuse, a pretext, for losing self-control. To lose such control individually is still to risk sanction, but to lose control in crowds of thousands lends immunity and even moral absolution to doing so. An individual on the street might be arrested for being drunk and disorderly, but not a thousand people. There is safety in numbers.

But why should anyone in Britain wish to lose, or at least to misplace, self-control? Why should anyone want so to lose, or misplace, his social inhibitions that he behaves foolishly, dangerously and unattractively?

We have already seen that self-restraint has changed from a virtue into a vice. A person who holds himself back is suspected of the crime of old-fashionedness, an opponent of the new way of being British, an enemy of the people.

The opposite of self-restraint is spontaneous self-expression. It is little wonder, then, that people should eat as and when they feel like it. On what other basis but personal inclination could they decide? Who, apart from the individual concerned, has the right to decide such a matter? Would not a society in which people did not have the right to make this choice be an intolerably authoritarian one?

It is a curious thing that those who are most in favour of spontaneous self-expression—the most perfect fit between inclination and performance—

should also be the most insistent on the power of formal rules to lay down the limits of human conduct. These limits should forbid as little as possible, of course, but within these limits everything is permissible. If the law permits me to do x, then no one can reproach me if I do x.

Otherwise, all social rules, being informal, are unenforceable and indeed illegitimate. Being the expressions of social power over the rights of individuals, such expressions of power are the means by which sectional interests defend their patch and control everyone else. Informal rules are not so much the lubricant of social intercourse, as the means by which one group dominates the rest. Clearly, therefore, informal rules must be broken as a mark of everyone's freedom.

Needless to say, it is not very easy to eliminate informal rules from social intercourse. Though you may sweep them out with your conscious mind. Yet they will return via you unconscious mind. Indeed, it is almost impossible to conceive of social intercourse without such informal rules.

To object to them as a category is like objecting to breathing or other bodily functions. No doubt life would be in certain respect more convenient if we did not have bodily functions, and we could save some time for more worthwhile activities thereby.

But nobody—quite rightly—gives a second thought to physiological utopianism. On the contrary, a great deal of human ingenuity has been expended on, say, the disposal of urine in such a way that huge numbers of people can congregate together in cities without being overpowered by a nauseating smell. If, by any chance, we enter a public building that smells of urine, we know at once that there has been a social breakdown in which rules are not adhered to and that we are likely to be less safe in it than elsewhere.

The question, then, is which informal rules conduce to a more civilised, decent and free life.

But what of the rule against eating on the street? On what grounds could we justify it?

The fact that disobedience to this rule (so wide that it can almost no longer be called a rule at all) leads to littering of the streets is a purely contingent one. The one doesn't necessarily lead to the other. It is surely possible that people should eat on a street and yet not litter it. Indeed, it is likely that many, or at least some, take their litter home with them, or use public trash cans. And what is possible for some should be possible for everyone. Thus there is no essential or inescapable connection between eating on the street and litter.

Perhaps this is so. But in the same way there is

no essential connection between carrying a large knife and stabbing people to death. It is perfectly possible for a person to carry a knife for the duration of his entire adult life and never use it to inflict injury on anyone with it. The Sikhs are a notable example of this possibility. It is said that, in the poorest areas of our cities, a very large and growing proportion of the young population carries knives for its own protection. But even now the number of stabwounds inflicted is very much smaller than the number of people regularly in a position to inflict them. Indeed, it would be possible to argue that, in the social conditions in which the most vulnerable to knife-attack live, the prevalence of knife-carrying actually lowers the rate of stabwounds, since it equalises the chances of a would-be assailant ending up with a serious wound. Knife not that ye be not knifed is the new moral injunction.

Yet we do not see much objection to laws against the carrying of offensive weapons in public, unless one has a good and specific reason to do so.

There is no essential, though there is a meaningful, connection between drunken driving and road accidents; or between drunkenness and violence. The great majority of people who drive while drunk will not cause an accident, though their uncoordination (the degree of which varies to an extent from person to person) makes them many times more likely to do so. There are people who argue that it is unjust and tyrannical to convict people of a crime before they have actually caused any harm to anyone, as is the case of the great majority of people convicted of drunken driving, or even of merely sitting in a drunken state at the wheel of a car; but most people would accept that, in this instance, the trade-off between the loss of liberty and safety on the roads is worth accepting. If everyone were left to himself to decide whether he was a safe driver when he had had a few, the frequency of drunken driving would undoubtedly increase, such is the partiality of men's judgement in favour of themselves. The numbers of deaths caused by drunken drivers would increase; and it is unlikely that any severity of *post facto* punishment of such drivers would affect very much the propensity to drink and drive.

We should not delude ourselves that the prohibition of drunken driving does not represent a loss of liberty: it does. But liberty is not the only thing we cherish. For myself, I am willing to forgo the freedom to drink and drive in exchange for a much reduced chance of being killed myself, or those I care for being killed, by a drunken driver. I concede that others might think differently and I cannot prove that they are wrong to do so. The question of where to draw legal limits is always one of judgement, not of Euclidean proof. And judgement is, or ought to be, affected by the particular circumstances in which it is made, both in time and in place. If the roads were much less crowded than they are now, if not many people habitually drank to excess, if the chances of a drunk driver killing a third party were much lower than they are now, then the loss to conviviality and coaxial life that a rule against drunken driving entails would be a price, perhaps, not worth paying.

The question of drunken violence is also instructive. We mostly take it for granted that the explanation of a brawl is that it was drunken. At the same time, however, we are perfectly aware that most people who drink, even to excess, do not fight. Indeed, the propensity of people to fight while drinking varies from culture to culture. It is greater in the slums of Glasgow than in the clubs of Pall Mall (though not unknown even there). Patterns of drinking matter more than the total amount drunk. Thus the social problems—and, of course, the social benefits—caused by drinking vary from situation to situation. There is thus no universally correct response to the problems caused by drinking: all politics are local, and a locality may change.

It is no consolation, then, that there is no essential or inescapable connection between eating on the street and the presence of litter. In our present circumstances, there is; and that should be enough for us.

5

Barbarians

Britons now drop litter as cows defecate in fields, or snails leave a trail of slime. That is to say, they do it naturally, without conscious reflection.

Occasionally, however, this is not so. They make a choice to drop, or at least to leave, litter.

On the way to the prison in which I worked in the afternoons was a bus stop, next to which was a large litter bin. I observed with a certain horrified fascination the conduct of young people who approached the bus stop, snack in hand. They would pause near the bin, as if for thought. Then, after this pause, they would take the wrapping from their snack and drop it not in, but on to the ground very near the bin. They would then continue to eat their snack with a calm and satisfied air.

What accounted for this strange behaviour? It was not unusual, at least in the statistical sense, because the ground around the bin was strewn with a great deal of litter, often more than in the bin, and certainly more than in other areas of ground of equal size. Was the act of dropping the litter not in but near the bin a subversive act, a commentary on a society that the people who behaved like this believed had been unjust to them; had denied them that to which they thought they were entitled? It would not be very difficult to construct a case on their behalf against society, though it would be rather different from the one they would construct themselves. While they would complain of the unequal distribtion of wealth and goods (particularly luxury items), it was in fact the case that society had enclosed them in the environment of their birth by failing to make them aware that something else was possible for them, if they made an effort, and by failing to encourage them in anything but the continuation of their current way of life.

Be that as it may, when people believe, rightly or wrongly, that they have been the victim of large-scale or existential injustice, they do not perceive such small benefits as they receive from an unjust society as benefits at all. They will reject them, even to their own detriment. That is why, when public authorities try to provide amenities in the worst areas they are so often, and so quickly, vandalised. Such amenities are perceived by the inhabitants as a cheap bribe, or as crumbs from a rich man's table, carelessly, negligently and dismissively tossed in their direction to keep them quiet: more an insult than a benefit. A litter bin, embossed and painted, as this one was, with the city's coat of arms, was precisely such an amenity. By dropping litter near it, but not in it, the young people of the neighbourhood were letting the council know what they though of its condescending generosity to provide a system of collecting and removing their litter.

Or perhaps there was another explanation. Perhaps the litterers near the litter bin were like barbarians who had recently come to live in a city that was once a bearer of civilisation, but had been conquered by people of lesser sophistication. Barbarians who conquer seldom wish, after all, to destroy utterly the higher civilisation (occasionally they do), but to assimilate to it while remaining in charge. But because they are barbarians and do not fully understand what they have conquered, they do not reproduce exactly the behaviour or manners of the former civilisation, but a simulacrum, or a version mixed with their own less polished ways.

Hence young people with their snacks approach litter bins in the knowledge or half-knowledge that they have something to do with litter. Like Goths in Rome, though, they are not quite certain what. Thus litter bins are as magnets to iron filings. They draw litter to them, but do not pull it inside their entity. When the new barbarians see the litter scattered around the bins, they conclude that they are a mark for litter on the ground, and hence drop their own litter near enough.

Sheer laziness sometimes accounts for the dropping of litter. I recently saw a British businessman, well-dressed and prosperous, throw a small piece of litter into a bin at Lyon airport while waiting for his flight. The piece of litter hit the rim of the bin and fell to the ground. The man looked at it, thought about picking it up, and even made a slight wave at it as if he were about to do so. But then he decided against and walked on, though he was not in a hurry, for his flight was an hour later.

Civilised conduct is not a matter of intelligence, either, and perhaps not even one of formal education. In an area of London full of famed postgraduate educational institutions, I watched a young man with a backpack full of books, by his age almost certainly a PhD student in some abstruse subject that it would take a great deal of knowledge even to broach, pause before an array of four large litter bins, and then drop his litter on the floor. I did not intervene, to avoid the humiliation of an argument in public, or worse still a physical danger.

But all that is necessary for litter to triumph is for the tidy to do nothing. A friend of mine, seeing a young woman drop an empty cigarette packet in the street, picked it up and, estimating that he would be in no danger from her, returned it to her.

'Here,' he said, 'you dropped this.'

'Oh it's all right, thank you,' she said brightly. 'I've finished with it.'

To see my students wading, apparently unconcerned, through the mess of their own creation was something of an unpleasant shock for me. Of course, without actually asking them whether they minded it, I could not be sure of their contentment with it, but there was certainly no sign—for example, that a single one of them had cleaned up the mess in front of his own lodgings—of discontent. So much for the social conscience of the burgeoning degree classes.

Let us suppose, no evidence to the contrary being apparent, the students did not mind the mess, were quite content with it, in fact. What would be wrong with that? After all, nothing is good or bad but thinking makes it so.

The rubbish might be a health hazard, of

course. My medical students know, it might favour the breeding of rats, for example, by making their subsistence easier. Rats can spread diseases, from leptospirosis to rat-bite fever (bubonic plague is spread by the black, not by the brown rat). But whether, in any given situation, they do so is an empirical matter, not something that can be settled in advance. And I should be rather surprised if, in fact, rat-borne diseases, not very common, had increased significantly among the littering students.

Besides, the production of a health hazard is not enough in itself to justify the prohibition of a behaviour. Car accidents could not happen if nobody drove cars. It is only when the health hazards of a certain behaviour are considered so great, or the costs of suppressing it so slight, that action can or should be taken against it. This is a matter of judgement, not truth; and there is as yet little proof that the littering of our streets leads to ill-health.

It might be objected that the health hazards of littering, if any, do not, or at least would not, necessarily fall upon those who litter, but upon innocent third parties. But that is true of activities such as driving cars or mountaineering: it is by no means uncommon to hear of fatal accidents befalling the rescue teams of stranded mountaineers, for example, to say nothing of the costs involved.

At least the driving of cars sometimes has a serious social purpose, such as going to work. Littering is an activity that has no positive benefits for the person doing it, or for society as a whole, beyond saving the litterer the trouble or inconvenience of disposing of his litter in a tidier manner. To his own way of thinking, however, this inconvenience might be great. It might even interrupt his social life, the most important aspect of his whole existence. By what right does society demand that he should forgo his pleasure? Is it not merely a more refined form of sadism than the infliction of pain?

But litter is unsightly, it spoils the appearance of the place in which it is dropped or scattered. And there are few places so ugly that they cannot be made uglier. Anyone who doubts this should compare the appearance of a poor area on a bright and an overcast day.

Unfortunately, unsightliness — like all aesthetic judgment — is in the eye of the beholder and this provides no objective criterion of permissibility. The fact that I am distressed by the litter everywhere to be seen in Britain is a fact of my psychology, and not an 'objective' one about the state of Britain. (Of course, if there were in fact no litter in Britain, I would be hallucinating.) As the students demonstrate, it is perfectly possible to see what I see and not be distressed by it. More interestingly, it is possible to see it and not to notice it. 'You see, Watson,' said Holmes, 'but you do not observe.'

It is perfectly true that one fails to remark on what one grows accustomed to. The constant stimulation of a nerve will soon have an attenuated effect. We have all had the experience of entering an enclosed space in which there was an unpleasant smell, only to find that after a little while we can smell it no longer. This surely offers us grounds for hope, of a kind. Once somewhere has become littered enough, and for long enough, we will simply fail to notice it any longer, it will cause us no distress, and no harm will have been done in the long run.

Ugliness, no less than beauty, is in the eye of the beholder. It is only necessary, therefore, to retrain the eye of the beholder for the hideous to become beautiful: and *vice versa*, of course.

After all, taste changes. Subsequent ages are able to see what was not apparent to earlier ages. People who might once have laughed at Picasso now pay large sums for the off-scourings of his production, and I do not think they do so for reasons of social prestige alone, though it no doubt plays a part.

The aesthetic opinions of the educated change fastest of all. Let me give one small example. In the 1930s, Evelyn Waugh, an educated man who was not completely insensitive to visual beauty, could see no merit at all in the aesthetics of the Ethiopian Orthodox Church. In fact, he thought that church laughably primitive, and I have little doubt he thought so because of what he considered the innate inferiority and incapacity of Africans, for whom he displayed no human sympathy whatsoever. When, sixty years later, I saw an exhibition in Paris of Ethiopian illuminated manuscripts and other religious artefacts, I was deeply moved by their beauty.

I do not think my response, so different from Waugh's, was simply a reflection of my superior powers of appreciation, thanks to some innate merit of my own. Indeed, I could not actually refute, with a knock-down argument, anyone who agreed with Waugh's judgment. I think Waugh was an authentically horrible man, mean-spirited, vicious, lacking in imaginative sympathy, arrogant and cruel, but that does not make the artefacts of the Ethiopian Orthodox Church any the more beautiful. There is a difference between aesthetic and moral judgment.

What, then, is the source of the difference between Waugh's judgment and my own?

In the first place, I was born nearly half a century after him. The potential moral consequences of dismissing large segments of humanity merely because of their racial difference from oneself had become only too clear, in a way that perhaps they had not been in Waugh's childhood. And if one could not dismiss whole races as innately inferior, one was much more likely to look upon their productions with an open mind, without the supposition that anything they made must be of negligible quality, belonging, as it were, to the childhood of mankind. One was therefore open to the possibility of beauty in unfamiliar places, and this (it seems to me) was a moral advance, if one that had been dearly bought.

Second, I had an Ethiopian friend at medical school. Actually, he was Eritrean, but Eritrea was still part of the Ethiopian Empire then, and he displayed no inclination to nationalism. He was a remarkable young man, far more remarkable than any of us gave him credit for, wrapped up as we were (and, knowing little of the world, as youth is inclined to be) in our own world. He had been a shepherd in Eritrea, but had gone to a mission school where he showed exceptional promise. Through the missionaries, he heard of scholarships to England, founded by the eccentric headmaster of a well-known public school who had an exceptional interest in Ethiopia; they were awarded every year by examination in Addis Ababa. He walked there, took the exam, and was awarded a scholarship. He showed us the black and white photograph of him receiving the award from the hand of the Emperor, and though of course we affected the disabused attitude that youth mistakes for sophistication, we were secretly impressed because he was the only one among us who had shaken hands with a world figure.

He was dignified, modest and humorous. He had experienced more, and known more, than any of us, of course. He had made the transition from shepherd in a desert land to medical student in a cold climate with astonishing ease and grace. We went on holiday with him to Ireland, hiring a horse-drawn wooden caravan, and he taught in the lanes of Ireland us how to make toothbrushes out of twigs. He sang Eritrean shepherd songs as we jogged along, and it is of him that I think when I think of inner strength. He laughed without bitterness, and with genuine amusement, when a boy in rural Ireland, which was then still far from multicultural, touched his skin to see if the black came off.

A single bad experience of a member of a

human group is often enough (psychologically enough, that is) to predispose someone against it as a whole; the reverse is also true, and because of my friendship I was never able to read Waugh's casual dismissal of Ethiopians without deep disgust. And this in turn predisposed me to find merit in Ethiopian art.

Finally, the manuscripts and other artefacts in the exhibition in Paris were displayed in such a way as to enable one to concentrate wholly upon them as objects in themselves, free from extraneous or distracting circumstances. It was unlikely that Waugh had ever had the opportunity (or probably the inclination) to see them like this. It is easier to see beauty in something when it is pointed out to you.

Still, Waugh's judgement seems to me not merely mistaken, but banal and lacking in intelligence. After all, many of the exhibits belonged to the British Museum or the Bibliothèque Nationale, and were collected long before Waugh's time, implying that at least some men of a previous age were more perceptive than he. What I rather feared, however, was that, had I lived in Waugh's time, I might have formed the same judgment as he.

All this goes to show that aesthetic judgment is fragile and changeable, susceptible to influences that are not primarily aesthetic in nature. When, therefore, I signal my distress as seeing a landscape littered, I am not sure how I would answer someone who said to me, 'Oh, come, come, it's not so bad, the litter occupies only a small part of it,' or even, 'Well, I think it adds something to it.' I am not sure I would believe in the sincerity of my interlocutors, for there is in practice rather more agreement in aesthetic judgment than I have suggested, but I should still be at a loss to know what to say. There are plenty of other aesthetic judgments that seem to me to be perfectly obvious—the brutal hideousness of the vast majority of contemporary Anglo-American popular music, for example—but I am clearly outvoted on most of them.

However, I suspect that those who are not outraged by or distressed at the litter that now submerges Britain's towns and countryside do not so much like it as fail to notice it. And this is only in part because they have grown so used to it that they think it is natural, as much a feature of the land as oxygen is of the air (in fact, they are probably more concerned about the composition of the air than about what is under their feet).

Of course, to realise that the littering of town and countryside is not natural, it is necessary to realise that things could be different. And this requires either memory, in the case of people old enough to have lived at a time when things were different, or imagination fed by historical knowledge. Comparison with other countries, and therefore foreign travel, might serve the same purpose, at least in theory.

The memory of people who lived at a time when there was less litter is easily dismissed as golden-ageism, the propensity of the elderly to invest the past with a glow of perfection. A more sophisticated version of this dismissal is indissolubly to associate the superior aspects of the past with its defects, as if, for example, the cleanliness of the streets were just the obverse of the awfulness of the food at the time, as if there were a choice between good food and dirty streets on the one hand, and bad food and clean streets on the other. Babies exist to be thrown out with the bath water.

As to those too young to have known anything but public slovenliness, they have been carefully and deliberately prevented from developing any sense of the past; they do not even know what it is to have such a sense, or that it is necessary. For what use could it serve? Would it increase their chances of getting a job, could it increase their income? It is as if the words that end the first part of Hume's *Enquiry*, in which he ironically deprecates all written works that treat neither of mathematics nor or of scientific experimentation, had been written about the study of history:

> If we take into our hand any volume; of history, for instance; let us ask, Does it contain anything that will help me procure a job? No. Does it contain anything that will increase my earning power? No. Consign it then to the flames: For it can contain nothing but sophistry and illusion.

The destruction of any sense of the past, and of the importance of the past, serves the ends of those people who believe that humanity, unsatisfactory as it is, requires remoulding by them, so that it will take better shape in the future. This is for its own good, of course, at least in the long run, but in the meantime the moulders must be granted if not plenary, at least extensive powers—which, as it happens, usually entail a generous share of the good things of this earth, for clearly it would not be right that the people engaged upon such important and hazardous work should themselves have to fret over such trivia as the standard of their own living. They should not be distracted by discomfort.

Humanity, then, should be regarded as a *tabula rasa*, the blank slate upon which Mao Tse-Tung said that such beautiful characters could be written. In so far as any awareness of the past is to be permitted, it should be as a terrible prelude to the present. It is therefore not a coincidence that the teaching of the Atlantic Slave Trade and of the Holocaust should play a preponderant role in the teaching of history in schools (though whether the Holocaust came before or after the Slave trade it is not necessary to know), in order that the beneficence of the present rulers should be understood. No other sense of history is necessary; indeed, it is actively unwanted.

And it must be admitted that if there had been a centralised conspiracy to deprive a population of any sense of continuity with the past, other than as an obstacle to the fulfilment of present desires, no conspiracy in the history of the world has been more successful. Never before has an entire generation floated so freely in the present moment.

Interested in the mental world of my young patients, I would enquire into their knowledge of history. For example, I would ask them to name a British Prime Minister other than the present one and Mrs Thatcher (memory of her survives as a kind of wicked-witch figure, half-believed in). The usual answer was, 'I don't know, I wasn't born then,' as if nothing could be known except by personal acquaintance. The words *Ten sixty-six* were more likely to evoke the price of a CD than of an historical event of some magnitude.

Now of course, even under a better dispensation with regard to the teaching of history, it is very unlikely that there would be any mention of litter. No one would inform children that, once upon a time not so very long ago, the whole country was not covered with the leavings of countless millions of snacks. It is not any particular judgment that is made impossible by the failure to teach history. It is the capacity to, and the habit of, making judgments at all that is destroyed, or rather never developed. All judgment, said Doctor Johnson, is comparative. If you deprive people of any knowledge on the basis of which they might compare, judgment itself is rendered impossible. A non-judgmental population is the result. A population, living in an eternal present moment from which nothing ever could ever be any different even as it changes, that is putty in the hands of politicians and bureaucrats. At least, until that population suddenly becomes angry about something.

A people who have not learnt the art of reflective comparison do not go abroad to learn or even to see. They go abroad to do exactly what they would do at home if they could, seven days a week instead of two (the weekend), in greater warmth and sunshine. They have no interest in the local customs or history. They take their own way of life with them, as if there were no other possible, and exaggerate its most unattractive aspects.

Though they must have heard multicultural pieties, it does not occur to them that the people to whose countries they flock might be offended or repelled by the behaviour of their visitors. There is a logic in this. If it is really true that all cultures are equal and all customs are therefore acceptable, then nobody has the right to criticise theirs or deem them despicable.

Anyone who has seen young Britons gather in foreign holiday resorts will vouch for the following. They enact scenes of drunken debauchery every day of a kind that second-rate Hollywood directors might arrange for cheap depictions of Sodom and Gomorrah. They drink, scream, fright and vomit in the streets; they think it right to shed whatever few remaining inhibitions they might have, and it is the duty of the host country to put up with it.

They are arrogant and uncompromising. They may not be very rich individually, but they are perfectly aware of their aggregate purchasing power and of their economic importance to their unfortunate hosts. There is therefore no reason why they should moderate their behaviour. I have watched Spanish policemen survey with disgust scenes of British debauchery that they surely would not permit their own people. Unhappy the resort that depends for its livelihood on mass tourism of the British young, who think that everything short of murder is permitted them.

It is not to be expected that the young British holidaymaker of this type will observe the difference in point of litter between his homeland and the country to which he has travelled. He has not come to observe, let alone to leer: he has come to indulge in his grossest appetites as fully as possible. And if you listen to such young Britons discussing the wonderful time they had the night before, you will discover that the irrefutable evidence they provide for the assertion is that they can remember nothing whatever of it, thanks to the amount that they drank. This is, of course, a rather dismal or pessimistic view of the pleasures available to human consciousness: and I often wonder, when I hear the screaming and shouting of drunken young Britons, whether there is not an undercurrent of desperation in it, the desperation of people whose lives are shorn of real meaning or purpose.

6

It's My Right

But, it will be objected, not all Britons, not even all young Britons, are like this. Certainly not. But it is not necessary that they should all be the same to have an effect on, or even set the tone of, society as a whole. If only twenty per cent of the population were inveterate litterers, for example that would be quite sufficient to submerge the country in litter.

Nor is it sufficient to understand a trend merely to take a poll or conduct a survey, and conclude that all is well because the people who hold loathsome views or behave badly are still in the minority. As far as can be ascertained from the results of free elections, a majority of Germans were never in favour of Nazism. A static snapshot of a society is not a good way to understand it.

And there is little doubt, I think, that the litterers among us have been in the ascendant for some time. Furthermore, they exert a kind of guerilla effect upon the non-litterers, as all people in Britain who indulge in bad behaviour exert such an effect upon those who do not. Those who still comport themselves with a degree of decorum are afraid to request, let alone demand, the same from their fellow-citizens.

Where does this fear come from? In part it is rawly physical, but it is also subtly metaphysical. Let us first consider the physical aspect.

People are afraid to request a modification of their fellow-citizens' conduct because they are only too aware of the fragility of their fellow-citizens' temper. There is nothing more to the social contract these days than an agreement to leave each other alone, whatever the other may be doing. The contract is enforceable at knife-point, and the highest principle is, *Noli me tangere*, don't touch me.

An awareness that so many young people carry knives is coupled with an awareness that those who are most likely to use them are precisely those who behave the worst or who make the most nuisance of themselves. However much you might be attached to clean streets or to a lack of intrusive music on trains and elsewhere, you are unlikely to want to die for the sake of these aims. Martyrs these days die only for bad causes.

It is clear, then, that minor anti-social acts

flourish because few people are willing to take the small risk of serious harm to themselves in objecting to them. Moreover, those who would be most inclined to object to them are precisely the people who, still retaining something of the former culture of self-restraint, are most likely to be embarrassed by public displays of emotion such as a request to someone to modify his behaviour—to stop dropping litter, to turn his music down, to take his feet off the seat opposite him on a train—is likely to provoke. For even if the person rebuked by a request to desist from something has no knife, or has a knife but does not exhibit it, he is likely to react with the vehemence of the justly-accused. And the last thing that a person of the old school wants is 'to have words' (to use an old-fashioned expression) with a complete stranger, especially when consistency would require that he would have to repeat the episode many times a day, each time with someone else physically much stronger than himself.

But that is not the end of the matter. The question arises as to why so many people, especially among the young, are now so easily moved to defensive anger, why they are so prickly, why they flare up so rapidly at any suggestion of reproach, however mildly couched? This rage, lying just beneath the surface like molten lava waiting to erupt, exists at younger and younger ages. Certainly if they are in groups, citizens think twice about speaking even to eight or nine year-olds. I confess that when I see bands of them in the street or on a bus, the image that comes to my mind is of a shoal of piranha fish.

The cause of this anger, of this exquisitely tender and inflamed ego that is like a bulging abscess when you press upon it, is an exaggerated individualism. Not only are people brought up to believe that their whim is law (many parents used to come to me in a state of puzzlement about the unpleasant conduct of their child because, as they put it, 'we gave him everything he wanted,' and even anticipated his future wants), so that the slightest frustration of their whim is experienced as suffering, but moral discourse has increasingly been reduced to questions of the rights of the individual.

The notion of rights, at least when carried beyond the broadest generalities contained in the American Declaration of Independence, is highly inflammatory to weak minds. There are, of course, philosophical problems with even the rights enumerated in the Declaration. If they were self-evident, why did it take so long to discover them? The self-evidence of a proposition is itself rarely self-evident until someone points it out. Self-evidence, in other words, is usually *a posteriori* rather than *a priori*. And could the existence of anything that was self-evident be denied or contested? Bentham was probably right when he called talk of rights 'nonsense on stilts.'

The speed with which an ever-expanding doctrine of rights has been generally accepted is astonishing (at least to me). It is not merely unquestioned, but unquestionable. I once asked a 17 year-old patient of mine for her ambition. She told me that she wanted to be a lawyer and I asked her whether there was any particular branch of the law that particularly interested her.

'Human rights,' she replied, with a beatific smile playing on her lips, as if she were a pious girl announcing that she had a vocation. Though she did not know it yet, here was philanthropy and five hundred per cent.

'Oh yes,' I said, 'and where do human rights come from?'

She looked at me with horror, as if I had committed a terrible social *faux pas*.

'What do you mean?' she asked.

'Well,' I said, 'are they there to be discovered, as Columbus discovered America, or are they made up as Hans Christian Anderson made up his stories, or are they merely granted by governments, in which case they may as easily be abrogated by governments?'

'You can't ask that,' she said, as if in pain.

I did not press the matter further, but suffice it to say that I did not expect my scepticism to have much effect upon her faith, a mixture of youthful idealism, self-righteousness and shrewd (if subconscious) assessment of career prospects.

The population, however, has no doubt about the metaphysical origin of human rights: they are inscribed in the constitution of the universe. A right cannot be abrogated, for then it would not have been a right in the first place; nor can it be hedged around by any kind of restrictions, for then, too, it would not have been a right. If I have a right to play my music, I have it here and now, at any volume I like. If someone within hearing of it claims his right to silence, the difference between us can be settled only by a contest of competing ruthlessness in the claiming of our respective rights. It is not surprising that in this context it is usually the most violent person who gets what he wants. People who are endowed with rights—and almost every day we hear of new ones—are naturally inclined to think of themselves as supremely important beings. First the heliocentric theory of the solar system, and then the theory of evolution, may have knocked man off his self-erected pedestal, but the doctrine of human rights has put him back there, but with this difference: that whereas it was once mankind in general that was on the pedestal, now it is every individual personally who is on it.

A person who is aware that he is endowed with rights, beyond the very elementary ones, develops certain characteristics. He becomes self-regarding. When his rights become extensive enough, when the encompass most aspects of human existence, he is deprived of the experience and therefore the attitude and expression of gratitude: for everything that he has, he has by right and is therefore merely the fulfilment of an entitlement. If, on the other hand, he believes himself to have been deprived of what is his by right (and the more extensive his rights, the more likely he is to feel like this), he feels aggrieved. The person endowed with rights therefore oscillates between ingratitude at best, and resentment at worst.

It is in the nature of man that disappointment should accompany him on his earthly journey; but when disappointment is felt also as an injustice, rather than as an inevitable consequence of having been born and self-conscious being, it is doubly painful. When you are told that equality of opportunity is your right, and that it is your right also to achieve anything of which you are capable, and when you compare these promises with your actual station in life, you are likely to feel cheated. For who, really, achieves his potential? Who could not have done better, if only things had been different?

Self-importance, together with a sense of injustice having been done to one, is not a recipe for easy sociability. Anger and bitterness are never far below the surface; and since one's own dissatisfaction with life is believed to be the consequence of one's rights having been violated or denied, the apparent happiness or good fortune of others is also the consequence of an unjust world. In fact, they are to blame. Thus the world is full of provocations on every hand, and rage is only awaiting an occasion to express itself. The slightest frustration caused by another person is felt as a challenge to one's rights that must be met and faced down, or else one will lose one's absolute sovereignty altogether. The distinction between respect and fear is erased. To be respected is to arouse fear in others.

Any form of correction, however mildly phrased or studiously restrained, is thus an assault on a person's conception of himself as the Sun King of his own soul. He will not accept any standards but his own. He may, of course, accept force as a reason for conforming to a rule laid down by others, though probably with resentment in his heart, but the moment the rule is no longer enforced efficiently he feels no reason to abide by it—quite the reverse in fact—for he lives in a culture in which non-conformity is now taken as the indication of independence of mind and spirit. It does not occur to him that non-conformity soon turns into a conformity of its own. The dithyrambs of John Stuart Mill to non-conformity as the source of all truth and progress are well-known to him, not because he has actually read great tract on liberty with attention, but because they have entered the general stock of conventional ideas. By contrast, James Fitzjames Stephen's riposte to Mill, that independence of mind does not consist of thinking differently from everyone else, but of thinking for oneself (which, of course, is impossible ninety-nine per cent of the time even for the ablest people) has not entered public consciousness. Nor, for that matter, has Mill's opinion, in the very same tract, that men who do not fulfil their responsibilities to the children whom they father may rightfully be put to forced labour.

So if truth and virtue arise from unconventional opinions and what Mill calls 'experiments in living,' does it not follow that he will be most truth-discovering and virtuous who departs most from convention?

Actually, it does not follow either in logic or in fact. It does not follow because a man who avoids one vice may easily fall into another: it is easy to avoid greed by the exercise (if that is quite the word) of sloth. And, as Mill himself recognised, many conventional truths are accepted as conventions precisely because they are true. We do not waste our time trying to prove, from the evidence we have gathered ourselves, that the world is round rather than flat, or that the blood circulates. The person who believes himself to be, and prides himself on being (the two things usually go together), highly unconventional daily accepts vastly more conventions than he could ever challenge.

It is political beliefs and social conventions that the 'unconventional' person usually challenges. Scientific geniuses like Richard Feynman, unconventional in his scientific ideas and, mildly so, in some of his behaviour, are so few and far between as to be sociologically or demographically insignificant. And even here things are not straightforward, for often those who believe themselves to be bravely attacking a convention are attacking what has long ceased to exert any serious hold on people. For example, several prominent intellectuals recently published within a short space of one another polemical attacks on religion, both from the philosophical point of view and the point of view of religion's actual effects in history and on the world today, often using arguments that date back to Lucretius, arguments that were familiar to me by the age of twelve or thirteen. (My father possessed many of the books in *The Thinker's Library*, published by the Rationalist Association, bound in brown with a blind-stamped representation of Rodin's statue on the cover, amongst which was a collection of essays by Charles Bradlaugh, the evangelical atheist of the second half of the Nineteenth Century and first avowedly atheist Member of Parliament, who used to stride on to a public stage, take out his pocket watch and challenge God to strike him dead in sixty seconds.) The new intellectual atheists, however, write as if they were brave pioneers, fighting an orthodoxy and taking their lives in their hands, as if they had shouted 'God does not exist and Mohammed was not his prophet' in the middle of Mecca during the Haj. Leaving aside the question of whether God actually exists or not, and whether religion has contributed or detracted more from civilisation (even assuming that to be a sensible question), it seems to me, an atheist, obvious that nowadays it requires more courage, at least in intellectual circles, openly to avow a religious faith than to deny the existence of God. For many centuries, of course, this was not the case: hence the eloquent ironies of Gibbon and Hume, who felt they could not come straight out with their own infidelity, but had to clothe it in a code. But the fact that the times have changed rather seems not to have obtruded even yet upon the minds of our modern atheists, who believe themselves to be living in intolerant theocracies.

I use this only as an illustration of the way in which people, often very clever people, as the new atheists are, may mistake what conventional belief actually is. Thus many people believe themselves to be flouting convention by behaving in a manner that was once unconventional, but is so no longer. There are now far more bohemians than there are men who go to work in three-piece suits and bowler hats, with a rolled umbrella. Generals, it has been said, always fight the present war as if it were the last war, but they are not alone in their anachronism. Whole populations may believe that they are being daring when they oppose what had long since been defeated or has passed away. This is particularly so once there has been a mass intellectualisation of society. Then millions of people may consider it their duty to reject the wisdom of ages, or at least of previous generations. To do otherwise would be to lose caste.

Hence, it would not worry young litterer to learn that that their behaviour represented a change from that of their predecessors. On the contrary, it would encourage them.

7

The Other World

Still, I suspect that if you drew the attention of such people to the litter with which their country was swamped, most would admit that it was unsightly. But it would come as a surprise to them, because previously they had not taken much notice of it.

The students walk through littered streets without noticing it not only because they are accustomed to it but because they are cocooned in a little world of their own. A high proprtion of them, when on their own, walk in the streets with headphones relaying music into their ears, the kind of music that induces a trance-like state. They spend an unprecedentedly large proportion of their waking lives, and sometimes even their sleeping lives, attached to or within perception of some kind of electronic stimulation. From a very early age, they are more familiar with the television screen than with the outside world (a high proportion of British children are no longer permitted by their parents to play outside, the dangers being considered by them too great to risk). It is a matter of pride, and not of shame, to many parents that they have provided their children with individual television sets in their rooms. Computer games and i-pods complete the division of the world into the virtual and the real, the former being infinitely more vivid and absorbing (and ultimately real) than the latter. It is now possible to achieve a state of mind akin to that pleasant half-dreaming, half-waking state that most of us enjoy for a time after we have slept well, acceding to full consciousness only with a jolting awareness of life's difficulties, for hours on end. Pop music is the opium of the people.

The bombardment by electronic stimulation is, in any case, all but inescapable. Many shops agitate their customers, and destroy their powers of discrimination, by playing loud, fast music with insistent rhythms. No wonder customers contract considerable personal debt in the process of buying trifles that give them momentary pleasure. Even in many bookshops, where you might have thought that silence would be a stimulus to purchase, the browser is not left alone with his thoughts, or with those of a book, but has his brain jangled with music. In bars and restaurants, in the concourse of railway stations, the waiting lounges of airports, in buses, in the back seats of cars carrying young children, in homes where the television is never switched off, and many other places, screens wink and flash, imperiously demanding attention even if the sound cannot be heard and the pictures are too fast-changing to convey any narrative.

So all-pervasive has such stimulation become that people now grow uneasy in its absence, that is to say in the presence of their own thoughts. Just as city-dwellers often find the intense dark of night in the remote countryside both surprising and disturbing, never having realised that darkness truly is the absence of light, so they now find silence intimidating. It used to be that, in hospitals, silence was regarded as, if not part of the treatment itself, at least an aid to recovery and rehabilitation. Now silence is so threatening to patients—though they stay in hospitals only a fraction of the time that they used to stay—that they have to be provided with entertainment at all times, from the moment of their arrival to that of their departure, even if it is by death itself. (Hospital waiting rooms are another place in which screens compulsorily stimulate, and I once arrived at my outpatient clinic to the sound of a cheerful advertising jingle, enjoining patients, that is to say potential litigants, to remember that 'Where there's blame, there's a claim.')

When people live long and intensely enough in a virtual world, especially since childhood, they become what would once have been called 'other-worldly.' Professors, at least in the popular imagination, were once absorbed in abstruse intellectual problems, and as a consequence were expected to be absent-minded; but the modern absent-minded live in soap operas, or in a trance induced by pop music. Is there any difference in the value of the two types of absent-mindedness? After all, the loss of self in both cases is something that mystics might approve; and I have often told my patients, many of whom had learnt the cant of psychobabble, that they needed not so much to find themselves as to lose themselves. Does it matter how?

There is a difference (I think) both as to how and why the men absorbed in intellectual pursuit and those who entrance themselves with pop music lose their awareness of their immediate surroundings. The one is active, the other passive; the first lose themselves for a purpose not entirely selfish, the second for reasons of self-absorption or self-obsession. Notwithstanding any personal ambition for fame, money or glory the absent-minded professor may have, he hopes to contribute something worthwhile and possibly lasting to the stock of human knowledge. The man who entrances himself with pop music is concerned only for himself. It is oblivion that he seeks because he does not know what to do with consciousness, and because he does not like the ceaseless responsibilities that it imposes. When awakened from his trance, therefore, he is doubly inclined to anger. First because it is from his disaffection or anger that he sought refuge in oblivion in the first place, and which survives the trance because the trance has done nothing to alter its causes, or rather pretexts; and second because he is roused from a more to a less pleasant state of being, and all deviations from happiness are for him further evidence of injustice having been done to him.

A person who values a trance state for its own sake, who seeks to enter it as often and for as long as possible, is not one who is likely to take very seriously such small obligations as that not to drop litter, for the sake of others and the immediate environment.

Driving long distances is another way to enter a trance-like state. Who has not had the experience of suddenly coming to himself while driving, apparently unaware of all that he has driven through and past in the last few minutes, but during which he might well have conducted complex and dangerous manoeuvres at high speed? Not only is the prolonged nature of long-distance driving conducive to trance, but a large percentage of drivers now drug themselves with music as they drive. A straw poll of the music they play that one could conduct on any busy urban street in the country suggests that they play precisely the kind of music that most effectively induces trance, heavy on monotonous rhythm but light on other musical content.

However, while a trance-like state may explain the indifference with which people contemplate, or rather fail to contemplate, the mess around them, and may increase the ease or thoughtlessness with which they contribute to it, it does not fully explain the origins of the mess. After all, there are longer distances, far longer distances, to be driven in other countries in which there is no such mess. Nor is there any reason to suppose that people in other countries listen less to their radios and CD players as they drive: though it has to be admitted that the musical tastes of young Britons are uniquely degraded (one has only to listen to the popular music of almost any other country to realise this). Besides, serious road accidents are less, not more, common in Britain than elsewhere, precisely the opposite of what one might expect.

The car is for many people the extension of their home. Indeed, for some it is more important than their home in so far as it is a public expression of their status. One often sees quite modest homes with immodest cars parked outside. And the inside of the car on the road is a space almost as private as any in the home, perhaps even more so, since it is usually free of the sexual partner and children.

The claims of the private sphere have expanded as those of the public sphere have contracted. It is not true, strictly speaking, that the economy in Britain has been privatised, since the state's share of total economic activity has rarely been greater than it is now. Furthermore, the weight of the state in regulatory matters is also greater than ever before, to the point of crushing many a private initiative. Laws pour from the government's presses like words from the mouth of someone in the manic phase of manic-depression, most of them without any parliamentary oversight, such that people have difficulty in keeping up with the regulations even in their own restricted fields of endeavour. It is almost as if private property were held by its owners only on government sufferance, or on the strictest conditions of usufruct.

As a *quid pro quo* for its intrusion into and regulation of the smallest details of economic life, the government has encouraged the genuine privatisation of personal morality. It has become studiously neutral, for example, in the matter of the manner in which men and women choose to associate and have children together, no longer favouring marriage. In fact, this neutrality, like that of the British government to the belligerents in the Spanish Civil War, is more apparent than real. For just as in the Spanish Civil War one side received vastly more military support from outside than the other, so the government, by subsidising what were once considered irregular unions has actually encouraged and promoted them, turning itself in the process into a surrogate father on a vast scale. This is pleasing, consciously or unconsciously, to the government and the very large class of its bureaucratic dependents: responsibility is the perfect justification of the assumption of power. And just as their ought to be no power without responsibility, so there can be no responsibility without its attendant power. Of course, governments are quite prepared, eager in fact, to exercise power without responsibility, just as they are willing to deny responsibility to divert the blame from themselves on to someone else when things go wrong. But in general they seek ever more pretexts for ever more power to interfere—for the good of the citizens, of course.

And it never ceases to find such pretexts. On the contrary, the more it seeks them, the more it finds. No profession is safe from the creeping tyranny of the new philosopher-kings. The government, responsible for the health of the nation, circumscribes and gradually eliminates the freedom of the medical profession, and tells it in increasing detail what must and must not be done; the government, responsible for the education of the nation, circumscribes and gradually eliminates the freedom of university teachers, and tells them what, how and how many to teach. To demonstrate their increasing productivity, professionals must spend an ever-greater proportion of their time filling in forms to demonstrate their increasing productivity; they have not only to comply with regulations, but prove that they have complied with regulations. And thus work, even that which was once so rewarding that it was largely its own reward, becomes a form of slow torture.

It is scarcely any better in the so-called private sector, for two reasons: first because the private sector is almost as subject to government regulation as the public sector, and second because in any case large private organisations tend to develop bureaucratic controls of their own. The need to make a profit, and the fact that it is almost impossible to hide for very long whether a profit has or has not been made, no doubt limits their Gogolian absurdity; if private companies operated the same way as government departments, they would soon go bankrupt. But there is still scope enough for depriving employees of any enjoyment in their work.

Even the self-employed are now so regulated in their activities—because the government, as ever-vigilant and benevolent guardian of the welfare of the population must ensure its protection from confidence tricksters, swindlers and incompetents—that they no longer experience themselves as sturdily independent. They are independent in name only: nearly the same weight falls on them as on everyone else.

Everyone who experiences this weight of governmental interference and regulation knows how little any of it has to do with its ostensible justification. A great deal of it is an employment scheme of otherwise unemployable scriveners. These scriveners are themselves both aware and unaware of their own redundancy (the human mind is an instrument of consciousness quite wonderful enough, when the motive is strong enough, to contain within itself propositions that are not only in contradiction to one another, but known to be so, without rejecting either of them.) Thus bureaucrats may be engaged upon the most ludicrous of tasks, which they know to be such, and yet comport themselves with sincere urgency and gravity, as if the future of something vital depended upon their work.

Six months after terrorists flew passenger aircraft into the World Trade Center and the Pentagon, I received a well-printed form to fill at the prison in which I then worked and had been working for more than a decade. Accompanying the form, I received a letter to the effect that should I fail to fill it within a few days, my employment might be ended.

The principal question asked on the form was whether I was now, or had ever been, a terrorist. I was to tick the box, yes or no.

I don't suppose it is necessary to elaborate at great length on the absurdity of this proceeding. It would be a very strange terrorist indeed who told the truth simply because he was asked. A legal friend of mine suggested that the question might have been framed in such a way because it is easier to take legal action against a liar than against a person who has practised the activity he has lied about. But if so, it only transferred the absurdity to a slightly different plane. The fact would remain that, legally speaking, it would be considered worse to lie about being a terrorist than actually to be one.

The form, of course, must have given rise to something of a cottage industry, or rather several cottage industries. The senior civil servants must have met (perhaps over breakfast, to give themselves the impression that they were making sacrifices for the safety of the nation) to develop a response to the threat of terrorism. For the official mind there is no problem that does not have its equal and opposite form to fill, that will at least absolve officialdom of the blame when the problem is not solved.

Having designed and printed the form, the civil servants had created a lot of work for their underlings, both locally and nationally. The locals would have to ensure that all the staff in their institutions filled the form, and to chase up all those who failed to do so. Nationally, of course, the information so gathered would have to be collated and tabulated. One thing would not have increased as a result of all this activity: namely the security of the country from the threat of terrorist attack.

But though the form was pointless from the perspective of any ostensible purpose, it was not therefore totally without function. We must disabuse ourself of the old-fashioned, and perhaps once-plausible, idea that the ostensible end of bureaucratic activity is its real end. By intimidating me (and, *a fortiori*, many others) into filling a form which they must have known that I and all the others would regard as fatuous in the extreme, merely so that I and they could continue without any difficulties in my and their current employment—a refusal to fill the form would have been taken not as a protest against idiocy but as a sign of sympathy with terrorism, if not worse— the bureaucrats effectively destroyed my, and their, probity. And it is far easier to control a workforce that has no probity than one with high standards. The price of independence is adherence to ideals of conduct, and the object of power-seekers is to force those who would be independent to abandon them, and to turn everyone into time-servers. Once everyone is in it together, no one can resist anything.

If the form asking me whether I was, or had ever been, a terrorist were an isolated instance of such humiliating idiocy, it would not matter very much. But it is far from an isolated instance; indeed, there is an almost exponential increase in such instances. It is as if the leaders of our society had read three authors and had take their dystopian imaginings for blueprints: Gogol for absurdity, Kafka for menace, and Orwell for mendacity and the corruption of language.

The most frequent oppression to what de Tocqueville called 'soft tyranny,' so difficult to oppose because it creeps up on you unannounced, as it were, so that no individual instance of it is worth opposing by personal sacrifice, and also because its ultimate source is so difficult to identify, is withdrawal into a private world, what the opponents of Nazism who did not leave the country called 'inner emigration.' There was the same response in the communist world by dissenters from the regime: energy was reserved to private life, while the public realm was that of lies and worse than lies.

In these circumstances, all that happens beyond the enclosed walls of a home or the closed doors of a car, or that has no reference to narrow personal concerns, lacks both reality and importance. The world is divided into them and us, the 'us' being a very small number indeed, sometimes only one. Who cares what happens in a world of lies, of bullying, forced acquiescence and dissimulation? Why should 'we' obey its rules or abide by its norms? We want as little to do with it as possible, to the extent of not even looking at it when we don't have to, so that we don't notice and don't care when the public space is degraded by litter. For the public space belong to a world from which we have emigrated; it has nothing to do with us, or nothing important beyond what it can force upon us.

8

The Camera's Eye

'There is no such thing as society.' With these infamous words, repeatedly torn out of context, Mrs Thatcher became the *bête noire* of all the philosophers of England, Scotland and Wales. Taken in isolation, her words seemed to an entirely atomistic view of people aggregated in a geographical space, whose only real relation to one another was the cash nexus, buying cheap and selling dear (or trying to). And indeed, Mrs Thatcher did sometimes give the impression of being a mirror-image Marxist, that is to say an economic determinist who thought that once the economy was set on its feet, in directly the opposite way to that of which Marxists would have approved, everything else would be added unto it. This impression that she gave was quite misleading with regard to her real effect upon British society, and on the littering of the entire country that was soon to develop.

She did not help to destroy concern for or even awareness of the public space by privatising the economy, but by managerialising the public administration. This is quite another matter.

Self-arrogated government responsibilities did not decline in any fundamental sense during her period in office. In some respects, indeed, they even increased. When unemployment soared, the government became directly responsible for the entire incomes, low as they were, of larger numbers of people than ever for a very long time. It never renounced its responsibility for the provision of healthcare, education, pensions, unemployment and other social insurance, and even housing for a third of the population (though it is true that private home ownership increased greatly during Mrs Thatcher's mandate.)

What did change, however, was the way in which public services were organised. Believing, no doubt correctly, that there was a lot of waste and inefficiency in the public services, believing, no doubt correctly, that on the whole privately-run businesses were more efficiently run, she concluded, wrongly, that introducing the methods of private business into the public sector would increase its efficiency. Unfortunately, she failed to understand that an indisputable measure of the success or failure that was available to private businesses, namely the balance sheet, was not available to publicly-run services. And this was an absolutely crucial difference.

In the public service, no measure of success or failure was readily available. This was not because no such measures were intellectually conceivable, but because the people doing the measuring were either the same people, or closely allied to the people, whose success or failure was being measured. Man being a fallen creature, truth in the abstract is not always his overriding goal.

Believing that management was a science independent of what was being managed, or for what purpose, Mrs Thatcher's government thought that the answer to the problems of the public sector was control by managers, who were specialists supposedly in nothing but efficient organisation. Of course, since these managers were but of flesh and blood, and no one could act from motives of public rather than private interest, they needed incentives in order to manage efficiently. And this meant, it goes without saying, that they had to be set targets to reach, for how else could their efficiency be measured? (Efficiency had to be measured, or else everything would slip back to what it had been before.) The managers, or their close institutional allies were allowed to decide for themselves whether they had reached the targets set for them. Not surprisingly they found that they had. Their rewards and perquisites—until recently, they had been rewarded in mush smaller numbers by a fixed and publicly-announced rate of pay—depended upon their reaching those targets. They also had an unprecedented degree of control over huge sums of money.

Thus the scene was set for the greatest looting of the British public purse since the Eighteenth Century: with this difference, that now the looting was entirely legal and above-board. And the way the looting could continue or even increase was for the public sector to retain or enlarge its share of total economic activity.

The government of the day saw an opportunity for continued rule in this and seized it with alacrity and skill. It understood how a vast vested interest, beholden to itself, could be created with a mixture of bribery, cajolery and threat, all in the name of the public interest. It also saw how an enormous system of commercial patronage could be conjured out of nothing, by awarding large contracts to consultancy firms for purely notional ends, firms that would, of course, object to nothing that the government did nor raise an alarm about what was going on.

A swamp of corruption resulted that was not

merely financial. It was far worse than that. The corruption was moral and intellectual, and therefore insinuated itself into the recesses of the soul, and manifested itself in the personality of the people. They lied and equivocated, and corrupted language itself, in order that they should continue to be allowed to feed at the trough. Once they had done so it was very difficult for them either to stop or to complain. You can lose your virginity only once.

A society in which everyone, from top to bottom, is on the make, in which the very laws and regulations encourage him in the rankest intellectual and moral dishonesty, and whose first magistrate for many years lost no opportunity himself to act in a seedily disreputable fashion (though apparently without any awareness that he was doing so, which was worse than outright villainy), is not a society in which people will readily conform themselves to a regulation that might inconvenience them even but mildly, if they are not actually compelled to do so. The whole idea of the public good is so besmirched by the corruption—economic, intellectual and moral— that it is impossible any longer to appeal to it. When you are harried, browbeaten, cajoled, bullied, pursued, threatened, bribed and surveyed by the state and its agencies, you have little have little inclination left over for obedience: least of all obedience to what one judge called the unenforceable. You have already paid your dues to society. Society can now look after itself. In the small sphere left to you, you will do exactly what you please, without regard to anyone else.

This is not the retreat of the state, but an expansion of it that is completely dissociated from any real public purpose, in the context of a culture of inflamed egotism. It is a poisonous mixture that leads to small but repeated acts of social nihilism, such as the disposal of litter in the street and in the countryside.

Society, in the form of the state, makes its demands, but because its demands are unreasonable and self-interested, it is deemed by the population to have no rights. Coercion, not consent, becomes the way in which it maintains itself.

But if public authorities have lost their legitimacy, this does not mean that anything is expected of them, quite the contrary. Children continue to expect a lot of their parents, perhaps even more of them, once they have realised their fallibility. And a government that takes between four-tenths and a half of people's income is *ipso facto* making a very large claim about its responsibilities. And if a state of affairs continues for long enough—in this case, high levels of taxation—it will come to seem natural, an ineluctable order of things. A parent may be hated or despised, but he or she remains a parent nonetheless. However many times the state fails, then, it is still expected to succeed, in the normative if not the predictive sense of expectation.

The state has deprived most citizens of the responsibility for arranging many of the existentially important aspects of life in the modern world, such as health care and education, on the sole condition, which is scarcely one that is negotiable, of paying his taxes. A person who lives in what some people call without irony 'social housing' retains the right to dispose of his knick-knacks as he wishes, but of little else.

There is little doubt that the provision or regulation of some public services has led to an enormous improvement in the quality of life (and not just of the poor, incidentally. Prince Albert died of typhoid fever because he drank London's contaminated water). No one would wish to return to the days before there were proper drains or sewers. But more and more of a good thing is not necessarily a better thing. At any rate, there comes a time when too many responsibilities have been handed to, or claimed by, public authorities. And people who have resigned too many of their responsibilities, or had them taken from them, eventually lose their will to exercise any responsibility. They lose their sense of agency; they drop their litter for the same reason that Luther made his speech at the Diet of Worms, they believe they can do no other.

In the days when I visited patients in their homes—rented from the city council—I would sometimes notice that the back garden was not far short of a rubbish dump. Broken bits of old appliances would lie in the overgrown grass along polystyrene containers of long-consumed hamburgers, rusting parts of cars, old torn clothes and dismembered toys.

Remarking as gently as I could upon the unsightliness of it all, I asked the householder in a genuine spirit of enquiry why she did nothing about it. The answer was invariable.

'I've asked the council, but they haven't come.'

Lest I be accused of snobbery, let me add that I think most litterers of a higher social class would return a not dissimilar answer regarding the litter they dropped: that it was the responsibility of the council to clear up after them, because that is what they are there for and what they are paid to do. Not very long ago I had a discussion with the deputy arts editor of a well-known British periodical about the mass public drunkenness now so prevalent in Britain. She said she could see nothing wrong with it, that the drunkenness was harmless pleasure. Somewhat at a loss what to say, I mentioned that such drunks often vomited in the gutter, to which she replied that it did not matter since the mess could be cleared up after them.

Having spoken to men who have strangled their best friend or impaled babies on park railings, I was nonetheless taken aback by what was said. I am not an egalitarian, and believe that no real equality can exist other than equality before the law. But not in my wildest imaginings did I expect to hear an intelligent, educated and cultivated person in Britain suggest that it was the duty of someone else to clean up the vomit of people who had simply declined to control themselves. By comparison with this notion, the existence of untouchables in India to clear away human ordure is reason and justice itself. At least such excrement is an inescapable fact of human physiology, unlike drinking to the point of nausea.

I found myself in the extraordinary position of having to think of supposedly 'rational,' that is to say consequentialist, reasons, why vomiting in the gutter in a public place was wrong, and this in privileged surroundings while being served refined and delicate food in the company of a cultural elite. Could I argue that vomiting in the street was a public health hazard? I certainly couldn't prove it, and vomit, like urine, is—give or take the presence of *Helicobacter pyloris*—sterile. That it was disgusting? But disgust is in the mind of the repelled, and John Stuart Mill has told us that we are not to forbid anything merely because we find it distasteful.

I could think only of Burke's words in his *Reflections on the Revolution in France*: 'What is liberty without wisdom and without virtue? It is the greatest of all possible evils, for it is folly, vice, and madness, without tuition or restraint.'

Perhaps *greatest* of all possible evils is an exaggeration, in the light of history since Burke wrote. Nevertheless, if one really has to prove from first, or indubitable, principles the wrongness of vomiting in public that results from a crude lack of self-control, the least that one can say is that the hold of civilisation is not strong.

No society decays in this fashion without a reaction, however. Again, Edmund Burke illumines the matter: 'Men are qualified for civil liberty,' he says, 'in exact proportion to their disposition to put moral chains upon their appetites. Society cannot exist unless a controlling power upon will and appetite be placed somewhere, and the less of it there is within, the more there is without. It is ordained in the eternal constitution of things that men of intemperate minds cannot be free. Their passions forge their fetters.'

The unwillingness of people in Britain to place moral chains upon their appetites, and therefore upon their conduct, has led, naturally enough (and precisely as Burke would have expected) to an increase in the controlling power from without. The British police, who only a few decades ago were still organised on the deeply humane principles enumerated by Sir Robert Peel, have come more and more to resemble an occupying paramilitary force, decked out in all the paraphernalia of physical repression, that seeks to control by intimidation. Notices appear everywhere telling members of the public to do this or not to do that, on the assumption that, left to their own devices, they will behave badly because they have no idea how to behave in a civilised fashion. One is greeted on one's very entrance into the country, at the immigration checkpoint, with a warning that aggression or violence towards immigration staff will not be tolerated and will lead to prosecution. (Since these notices are posted where only people with a right to residence in the country form queues, they are a commentary on the conduct expected of the citizenry.) Such warning notices are encountered even in institutions, such as hospitals, whose sole function is to bring succour to the population. After numerous threats against, and actual assaults upon, the staff in the hospital in which I worked, the police posted notices to the effect that, henceforth, assaults on staff in the hospital would not be tolerated, suggesting both that hitherto they had been, and that they would continue to be tolerated outside the hospital—suggestions that were, more or less, an accurate reflection of reality.

One of the consequences of the failure of the British population to place a controlling power on its appetites from within has been a huge increase in surveillance from without. Britain is undoubtedly the closed-circuit television capital of the world. A third of all CCTV cameras in the world are deployed in Britain, and it has been estimated that the average Briton comes within range of, and is recorded by, such a camera three hundred times a day. And certainly it seems to be the case that, whenever there is a particularly brutal or horrible murder committed in the public space, the police announce that 'the video evidence is being studied.' Nothing much can happen off screen in Britain.

Of course, the fact that such murders take place at all despite the near-ubiquity of cameras suggests that they are not by themselves a very powerful deterrent. It is always possible that, were it not for their presence, there would be even more murders on the streets. And in certain circumstances, the cameras undoubtedly exert a deterrent effect, at least on those who are fundamentally law-abiding. Anyone who has observed the way in which most drivers slow down when they know they are approaching a speed camera will agree. They slow down not because they have a sudden crisis of conscience about the dangers of driving too fast, but because they fear to be caught and fined and have their licence removed. Those who drive illegally, on the other hand, without licence or insurance, and possibly in stolen vehicles, have nothing to fear from the cameras.

The high prevalence of littering and other forms of disorderly behaviour also justifies the presence of cameras, for they offer the illusion, though not the reality, of control. Like most attempts at repression in Britain, the effect is more apparent than real because the cameras in themselves cannot enforce anything. It is true that cameras with loudspeakers attached have been tried, so that someone monitoring the screen can shout at the litterer, 'Hey, you, pick that litter up!', but the startling novelty of such an order would soon wear off once it is realised that the voice issuing it had no means of enforcing obedience. The camera would soon be answered back in no uncertain terms, with a rude gesture into the bargain. Indeed, it is even conceivable that cameras attached to loudspeakers could worsen the situation, as young people taunted the monitors of the screens by performing acts to provoke them to impotent fury. In any case, every screen could not be monitored; but even if it could, the problem of impotence would remain.

The peculiarity of the creeping authoritarianism of modern Britain—that Burke did not anticipate—is that authority seeks only intermittently to exercise its actual authority. It is as if the new authoritarians regarded surveillance as an end in itself, as if they were but voyeurs, or as if they were more concerned to create an atmosphere of control than exert actual control. This is because appearance is at least as important as reality, and the appearance of power and control is as gratifying as the substance of power and control. I strut, therefore I am.

I experienced this very forcibly in a British court recently in which I was giving evidence in the case of a mentally handicapped man who had committed a series of relatively minor sexual offences, that were nevertheless alarming to their victims. Outside the courtroom itself, in the atrium to all the courts in the building, patrolled eight policemen in flak jackets, armed with automatic weapons. In view of the police's record of shooting the wrong person, I did not find their presence altogether reassuring.

I went into the court to await my turn in the stand. The accused was already in the dock, though the judge was not yet in court. Next to me in the public gallery was a woman whom I soon realised was one of the victims, accompanied by a young man of unpleasingly aggressive visage and demeanour who was clearly her boyfriend. He began to threaten the accused, quite openly and at sufficient volume for all in the court to hear. He said he would get the accused when he came out of prison, and kill him. This was a threat that anyone who saw him would have taken seriously and literally. Certainly the accused was very frightened.

Everyone in the court knew what had gone on, including all the officers of the court. Nothing was done to stop him, let alone to seek his arrest. The extraordinary situation, then, was this. The heavily-armed policemen outside the court appeared as much to be protecting a man's right to threaten an accused in the very heart of the criminal justice system as protecting the system itself from outside attack. At the end of the case, the man left the court having learnt that the repressive apparatus of the state was certainly not directed against him, and was more for show than for use.

In the matter of litter, this is clear too. You commonly find notices in Britain threatening litterers with severe penalties, the most severe I have seen being a fine of £2,000. These notices are rarely unaccompanied by litter strewn around them, as if in sacrificial offering; certainly, no one expects the threats of punishment to be carried out. Neither the means nor the will are there.

But could they be there? Could repression alone make men more virtuous, at least where littering is concerned?

The conventional answer is no; laws alone will not lead men to virtue. No doubt this is true when one is speaking of virtue in general terms. We do not call a man virtuous merely because he fears punishment if he does not behave virtuously. A man who acts only from fear is as likely to obey bad laws as good ones. Nor would we want a life in which the law laid down our conduct in such fine detail that we could not but be good if we obeyed it to the letter.

But if law is not, and ought not to be, all

powerful, neither is it wholly powerless. If enforced, it can and does change men's habits, because an act or omission repeated often enough becomes a habit, embedded in men's character. Perhaps the clearest example of this transformation is in the city-state of Singapore.

I come not to sing the praises of this tiny country, but simply to remark upon its transformation. At independence, Singapore was a colourful and interesting place, but no one would have described it (outside its colonial purlieus) as clean. And the commonist explanation for its untidiness and dirtiness would no doubt have been the indifference of its inhabitants, Chinese, Malay and Indian, in matters of public cleanliness. Yet within a few short years, the city had become one of the cleanest in the world. There is little doubt that the strict enforcement of laws prohibiting various means of fouling the streets—the Chinese and Indians, for example, were world-champion spitters, appearing from the sound of it to draw up phlegm from the most remote parts of their body—quite quickly changed the behaviour, and eventually the character, of the inhabitants.

If the laws against the fouling of the streets in Singapore were now relaxed, or not so vigilantly enforced, it seems to me likely that it would be some time before they became as dirty again as they had once been. Indeed, it might take a generation who had never known those laws before they did so.

This is not the place to examine the virtues and defects of Singapore as a whole. Many people have derided or decried its social authoritarianism, and certainly the rigidity of its rules can startle visitors unaccustomed to them. Once I stood at a taxi rank there (you are not permitted to wave a taxi down directly in the street) and was surprised that no taxi would take me. I began to think that there was something more than usually repugnant about my person to account for this, but then a kind fellow-patron explained it to me. I was standing two feet to the right of what I should have been standing. As the Chinese taxi-driver put it to me, with the extreme eloquence and concision that those who have not fully mastered a language sometimes employ, 'Singapore very very law.'

Of course, the rigour and severity of the law ought to be proportional to the situation with which it is expected to deal. A tropical city-state with a large population and a small land area is perhaps not the best laboratory for leniency, especially if its dedicated to those aspects of advancement, such as economic growth, that are susceptible of statistical measurement. Laws have, perhaps, to be less severe in larger countries where the population is self-governing (I mean in the personal, not the constitutional, sense) and aware of the need for virtuous self-restraint. But the British, as they currently are, do not fit this description. On the contrary, they now regard a lack of self-restraint as both essential to health and as demonstrative of democratic sentiment. There could not be a people more worthy of strict laws applied with vigour.

Not that this will happen. One can easily conceive of the erosion of due process on the one hand (it is already happening), and the passage of theoretically draconian laws on the other, to give a part of the population the impression that the government is as concerned as it is about such and such a social problem; but the enforcement of such laws is quite another thing, practical leniency always triumphing over abstract severity. Seriousness of intent and administrative capacity are simply lacking.

As in so much contemporary British life, the public service is earnest without seriousness and frivolous without gaiety. All social problems are employment opportunities and little else beside: certainly, they are not to be ameliorated, let alone solved. The effect of draconian measures, if passed, would, of course, have to be measured. This would mean setting targets, and targets would necessitate information systems to decide whether they had been met, personal assistants to deputy directors (information services) would have to be recruited. In short, much would be done, and many people employed. But in the process the original intention would have been entirely subverted, and even forgotten.

There are already by-laws and regulations against littering almost everywhere. But they are never enforced. An unenforced law is a great delight to those who feel themselves oppressed by the law, for then they can have their revenge for the oppression without any consequences. In any case, if officialdom is worried enough about litter to pass laws against dropping it, why doesn't it come and pick it up itself? After all, that's what it's paid to do, isn't it?

Not in its own opinion, it's not. It is paid to do whatever tasks it sets itself. And such tasks as collecting litter, or even arranging for litter to be collected, are beneath it.

One of the reasons for this is the increasing level of education, or at any rate number of years of attendance at educational establishments, of those who comprise officialdom. Laudable as the collection of litter no doubt is, it is not work suitable for an educated man. And educated man, it goes without saying, deserves to be paid more that an uneducated one of the type who might be expected to clean up litter. Since the growth in the number of educated people requiring jobs in the public sector increases faster than the funding with which to pay them, large tax increases notwithstanding, it follows that employment in, and expenditure on, such unskilled tasks as cleaning the streets and roadsides of litter have to be limited and if possible cut back.

Educated people have to be found work more worthy of their talents, or at least their status, than keeping the streets clean, or indeed any other similarly menial task. Ensuring the reign of political virtue (which does not include the disposing of one's litter in a tidy fashion) is more appropriate to their level of intellection. Virtue is conceived as the apportionment of the spoils of society according the size of its component parts. We may have filthy streets in this town, but at least we have a bureaucratic commitment to equal opportunities.

In view of the important responsibilities that the authorities have conferred upon themselves, then, it is not altogether surprising that they have not the funds, manpower or energy left over to sweep the streets (to say nothing of the grass verges of motorways). Yet the population believes that the responsibility to do so is not theirs. Long gone are the days when working class people regarded it as a manner of honour to keep the stretch of street in front of their terraced house clean and free of rubbish. The photographs of working class women scrubbing their doorsteps each morning as a visible token of their respectability are of a culture that is now as alien and distant as any described by an anthropologist in the Amazon jungle or on the islands off the coast of New Guinea. We now look on such women with pitying condescension and mild amusement, rather than with respect and admiration. Nowadays, we count ourselves enlightened though we have half-returned to mediaeval times (at least as popularly conceived), when people emptied their waste from windows on the second floor on to the street below.

I see this only a few yards from my flat in London. An interesting, though no doubt unwitting, social experiment has been performed on the side of the street opposite to mine. New blocks of flats, not offensively out of keeping with the predominant architecture of the area (something which is rather unusual), were built there. Half of the flats were for private occupation (and cost £500,000 each), and half, identical in style and structure, for 'social' housing. In front of the flats are tiny communal gardens, not more than five feet deep.

It is possible to tell, merely from the state of these tiny patches of garden, precisely where private property ends and 'social' housing begins. The patch in front of the latter is strewn with litter of a kind suggesting that it was thrown from the window. No one, surely, would go to the trouble of walking there, and there only, to deposit soiled babies nappies? The concentration of polystyrene containers of take-away meals also suggests ejection from the windows, for if they were merely thrown away by passers-by, their total absence from similar patches in front of the privately-owned flats would be surprising. Of course, it is possible that someone clears them away from the patch in front of the privately-owned flats, but I have never seen him at work.

Moreover—and significantly—the street itself in front of both privately and publicly owned flats is liberally strewn every day with the containers of food eaten by people as they walk along. This suggests that people do not even have the mental energy to toss their rubbish over a low railing, but rather let it fall wherever they happen to be when they have finished.

9

Litter Studies

There is another possible explanation, I suppose, for the accumulation of the rubbish in the patch of land in front of the 'social' housing: that rubbish begets rubbish. Once people see that somewhere is strewn with rubbish, they lose any inhibition they might have had about littering is destroyed. This is a variation on the broken-windows theory of crime: that minor signs of disorder and neglect lead people to suppose that public authority has evacuated the area, and they are therefore encouraged to think that crime will go unpunished.

Certainly, this is the theory on which I acted when I lived in a rather beautiful Victorian church close in a city not famed for its beauty, and that was appallingly littered in general. Every night, when I walked my dog, I would pick up the litter in the close (which sometimes included used condoms), in the hope that the tidiness that resulted would give pause to potential litterers. On the whole I think it worked, though I cannot be absolutely sure. Certainly, the close remained much cleaner than the neighbouring streets, even after I had been away for a few days. But since my neighbours did likewise, and would not let the close deteriorate, my hypothesis remained unproved.

On my way to Glasgow, driving along the particularly littered stretch of road I mentioned at the start of this book, another philosophical question suddenly came into my mind. (From where—another part of my mind? If so, in what sense was that part of my mind 'mine?' If I was unconscious of it, in what sense was I responsible for it? I am relieved that I am not writing about the philosophy of mind, a subject far too difficult for me.)

My—or perhaps I should say 'the'—question was this. Why did I feel so strongly that, the filthiness of the roadside notwithstanding, I should not myself add to it by throwing litter out of my car. And I saw at once a possible refutation of utilitarianism.

The first notion to refute is that I felt so strongly because of a fear of being caught and prosecuted. The chances of being thus caught and prosecuted were negligible. The sheer volume of litter by the roadside was testimony to this. If people were prosecuted even a tiny proportion of the times they dropped litter, our courts would deal with nothing else.

Second, I could not have felt so strongly that I should not add to the litter because of any aesthetic consequences of doing so. It was far too late for that. It is a physiological law that a sensory stimulus is not perceptible below a certain proportion of an already existent stimulus. If you are carrying a hundred pound weight, you will not perceive an ounce when added to it, though you can perceive that same ounce if you are carrying nothing at all. Another scrap of paper, another cellophane bag, another plastic bottle, could not possibly have made any difference to the appearance of the landscape.

Thus my strong resistance to throwing litter from my car in these circumstances could not have arisen from any consideration of the consequences for me or the landscape.

Of course, a rule utilitarian might reply that reluctance arose not from the consequences of my individual act, but from the consequences of my act if my act were taken as a general permission for everyone to throw litter from his car. If everyone acted as I acted in this regard, it would make a difference.

I do not think that this will do either. It depends upon the supposed fact that if everyone threw litter from his car it would make an aesthetic difference, but this is by no means certain. Speaking only for myself, additional litter, even if perceptible, would not have added to my displeasure on looking at the landscape. Perhaps I am too perfectionist, but blots on the landscape— or townscape, for that matter—destroy whatever pleasure I might otherwise have taken in it. That, no doubt, is why I find the vandalism of British architecture and town planning over the last sixty years so acutely painful and depressing. They have left no view untouched, and touched none that they did not ruin.

Other people, of course, might react differently from me. They might consider two million pieces of litter twice as bad as one million, or indeed four times as bad. But even if nobody thought this, even if everyone agreed with me that further littering of this particular landscape could not increase the displeasure it evoked, still I would feel it very wrong to throw litter from my car. Neither act nor rule utilitarianism explains or justifies this.

What does explain it, then? Why should I feel something akin to a Kantian categorical imperative with regard to litter (in a way that I do not with regard to lying), such that I would not even litter a country to which I felt a strong aversion or enmity?

Where do more feelings such as this come from? There is a strong tendency to over-emphasise cognitive processes in the formation of moral judgments. Of course I do not want to discount such processes altogether, far from it, especially in complex matters that require many factors to be taken into consideration and appropriately balanced. But in the matter of dropping litter, or rather refusing to do so, something rather deeper—more primitive, if you like—is at work, at least initially.

We can see that this is so in the absurdity of the approach of certain schools to the problem. Schools are often foci of litter. Children are consumers of huge quantities of snacks and soft drinks, and throw the wrapping and containers into any area of grass around their schools. No doubt the situation is worsened by the decision of many schools to permit vending machines on their premises. The harm done to the children by this must surely outweigh the good done by the revenue generated for the school; few would argue that children are the best judges of their own nutritional interest.

An acquaintance of mine told me that he had read a headmaster's reply in his local newspaper to a complaint about his school whose pupils left immense quantities of litter everywhere. He had, he said, instituted 'litter studies' as part of the curriculum. That is to say, the school was trying to change the behaviour of the children by purely cognitive means.

There is, curiously enough, a parallel in the field of criminology. Recidivists in prison undergo psychological course to 'restructure' their thinking, as if there were something disordered with it in the first place. As if burglary, for example, were the outcome of uncontrolled irrationality, when it is easy to demonstrate (at any rate in current British circumstances) that it is an economically rational thing to do, at least for an alarmingly large proportion of the population. The proper question, then, is not why such and such a person repeatedly commits burglary, but why so many people in exactly the same circumstances do not do so at all, though it might well be in their economic interests to do so. Once again, the threat of punishment cannot explain it.

The children in a school that feels the need to teach 'litter studies' do not litter because the children are lacking information. They are neither visually nor cognitively impaired. They litter because they have not been socialised properly.

When I think of the origin of my own aversion

to littering—I speak now of my own refusal to litter, not of my distaste for other people's littering—I realise how little it had to do with rational argumentation. This is not, of course, to say that there is no rational argument against littering, only that such argument was not the origin of my refusal to litter. I do not ask myself, every time I have about me a piece of potential litter in a public place, 'Shall I throw this in the street, or shall I dispose of it in some other way?' Nor, having failed to ask such a question, do I rehearse in my mind all the possible *pros* and *cons* of throwing it in the street and, having weighed them up with the utmost care, decide against doing so.

The reason I do not throw the potential litter in the street is my mother. Because of her, it simply does not occur to me to throw litter in the street, not even for a fraction of a second. Good behaviour is as much a matter of prejudice and habit as of ratiocination.

Conclusion

While writing this essay, three further phenomena came to my attention.

The first is the presence of chewing gum trodden into the pavements of all British towns and cities, giving rise to what at first sight can be mistaken for a marbling effect. Very few inhabitants of British urban dwellers can be entirely unfamiliar with the unpleasant sensation of recently discarded gum, still soft, sticking to the soles of their shoes, and producing a faint suction on their shoes as they walk. The task of removing the gum from the underside of a shoe is a distinctly distasteful one. I recently had the still more unpleasant one of removing gum from the leg of my trousers, to which it had stuck when I let my leg touch the underside of the seat in a bus.

A brief survey of a stretch of almost any road in Britain frequented by pedestrians will provide evidence of hundreds of individual acts of disregard of the public space, that is to say of sheer egotism. No doubt the number of offenders is not quite equal to the number of patches of gum trodden into the stone, for no doubt there are repeat offenders. But the numbers of people who behave like this must be substantial, for there must be many millions of such patches of gum in the country as a whole.

No doubt also there are many chewers of gum who dispose of it in a more thoughtful, less asocial fashion. For myself, however, I cannot but see a chewer of gum without wondering how he disposes of it, just as one used to wonder what German men of a certain age did during the war.

The fact that chewers of gum who leave it on the pavement know that they are doing wrong is demonstrated by the fact that one sees them do it very rarely by comparison with the number of times it must be done. It might be argued that the deposition of gum on the pavement is not done surreptitiously, by analogy with the fact that one very rarely sees a dead wild bird, and yet one knows that all the wild birds around one die. Yet the fact that such patches of gum are most common precisely in the busiest streets does suggest that chewers make some efforts to hide what they do, which in turn suggests guilt.

I do not want to enter into a philosophical discussion into the ethics of chewing gum. Presumably those who chew gum derive some pleasure or benefit from doing so, otherwise they wouldn't do it; but to me, chewers of gum always look distracted, agitated or even menacing, like those who incessantly tap their feet on the floor (but worse). Certainly it is difficult to imagine anyone making a declaration of love while chewing gum, or giving an expression to a finer feeling. Indeed, it is difficult for a person chewing gum to give his undivided attention to another human being, or at least to give the impression of doing so. A chewer of gum can look many things—cynical, anxious, incredulous, brutal—but not, I think, tender, happy or refined. This, of course, may well be precisely the benefit that the chewer of gum seeks from his habit. The chewing acts like the warning to predators of the brightly-coloured poisonous insect. One might expect the chewing of gum to increase in proportion to the perceived aggressiveness of one's fellow citizens.

It might be argued that an aesthetic objection to a habit, being grounded upon nothing except personal taste, is not sufficient to justify prohibition of that habit, such as in Singapore (though, if my surmise about aggressiveness and the chewing of gum be correct, the very appearance of such aggressiveness is likely to increase either fear or the countervailing aggressiveness in others, which is not a merely aesthetic question). Be that as it may, the fact remains that chewers of gum impose costs upon their non-chewing fellow-citizens, for local councils are obliged to clean pavements with high-pressure water hoses, a very expensive business as well as a frustrating one, for the chewers of gum immediately return to the fray.

As a compromise between outright prohibition and supine acceptance, then, I propose a hypothecated tax on chewing gum, to be used solely for clearing the streets of this unsightly nuisance, the tax to be raised to permit sufficiently frequent cleaning to achieve a standard on randomly-chosen streets of one deposit of chewing gum per hundred yards. If this hypo-thecated tax resulted in chewers of gum disposing of their gum in some other unsocial way, then outright prohibition should be enacted.

The second phenomenon is that of small sand-bags that, relatively recently, have been employed to weigh down and secure temporary road signs at road-works. They are not used in France, for example, and it surely cannot be beyond the wit of man (indeed, it used not to be beyond the wit of man) to achieve this end without them.

What is most striking about the use of these sand-bags is that they are seldom removed when the signs that they are employed to weigh down are removed, but are left where they are, in piles by the side of the road. (Quite often, too, the signs themselves are abandoned to rust by the wayside a little further on.) It is almost impossible to go very far along a trunk road in Britain these days without seeing such sand-bags and rusting road signs—or at least, without them being there to be seen, which is not quite the same thing.

What does this signify? At the very least, it means that the people involved in road repairs, from the labourers to the managing directors of the contracting firms, take no pride in what they do, but regard it simply and solely as a means to an end: that is to say, a weekly wage or annual profits. They therefore do the minimum that they can get away with.

But why can and do they get away with it? It must be because the staff of the public authorities who employ the contractors suffer from precisely the same disease. They do not care either. Their work means nothing to them except as a meal and mortgage ticket. Their concerns have been entirely privatised.

The third and final example is the increasing number of plastic carrier bags — despite the campaigns by newspapers and the supermarket charge — that now appear on the outskirts of towns and cities, neatly tied-up and filled to bursting with rubbish, but abandoned (thrown out of car windows) by the side of the road. What does this signify?

Since I have not spoken to people who behave in this fashion, I must speculate. The fact is that in many municipalities the number and frequency of household rubbish collections has been declining fast. In the small and agreeable town in which I live in England, there is now one collection of household rubbish every two weeks. It is not difficult to imagine that households with children might generate more household rubbish than can easily or conveniently be held over so long a period. The temptation to dispose of the rubbish in another fashion must be strong, especially to those whose attachment to social virtues is not all that strong to begin with.

But why are rubbish collections growing more infrequent? It can hardly be because our local taxes are declining, quite the contrary.

The answer lies in the degeneration of the public service in Britain. Local authorities do not take seriously their most elementary (but unglamorous) duties such as the collection of rubbish. This is largely because they have taken on so many other duties, many of them more gratifying to them but frivolous and time-consuming. Moreover, the principal purpose of the public service is to serve the private ends of those who work in it, to secure their well-being, generous pensions arrangements. In the circumstances, declining services and increasing taxes are not only compatible, but to be expected.

Trace litter to its origins, and you soon encounter the knotty questions of political philosophy, political economy and even the meaning of life.